SPOKE SIX

Publisher & Editor:
Kevin Gallagher

Managing Editor:
Karina van Berkum

———

On the web: www.massspoke.wordpress.com

———

SPOKE SIX

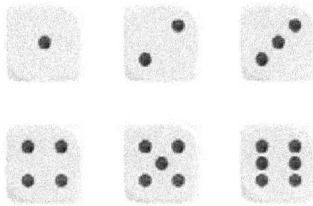

BOSTON, MASS.

SPOKE SIX

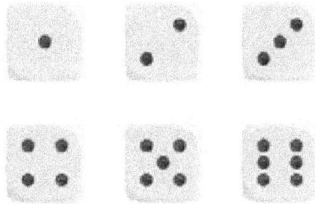

BOSTON, MASS.

TABLE OF CONTENTS

ESSAYS

INTRODUCTION

*"Against the ruin of the world, there is only one defense—the
creative act."*
Kenneth Rexroth

spoKe 6, continuing to advance:

1. A global poetry that engages with or is from the world's
places, cultures and literary traditions past and present.
2. American poetry that sees the English language and
literary tradition as core but only one of many roots and
paths for poetry.
3. A poetics that attempts to innovate language, idiom,
sensibility and poetic form while maintaining a public
presence.

In the spirit of one of Boston's greatest magazines, Cid Corman's
Origin, we give real exhibits of the works of one person or place in the
world. In the sixth spoKe we are happy to feature two of our region's
maverick poets in Amanda Cook and John Mulrooney. Once again
Paul Valente but this time with Ovid's love poems, and twenty Russian
Poets who had nothing to do with the US election.

We have a big bin of more poets, featuring Elizabeth Lund, Danielle
Legros Georges, Meg Tyler, David Blair, Marc Vincenz and more more
more from Sunnylyn Thibodeaux in San Francisco.

spoKe's first issue was a response to the Boston Marathon bombing.
Since then we have paid homage to some of Boston's most important
and often underappreciated poets. We have focused on Fanny Howe,
Damon Krukowski, Robert Creeley, John Brooks Wheelwright, Bunny
Lang, and more. In this issue we bow down to four who have left us in
in William Corbett, Gerrit Lansing, Sam Cornish, and Denise Lever-
tov.

There is more.

Kevin Gallagher
Publisher & Editor

FEATURES

LETTERS TO MAXIMUS / *Introduction*

Several years ago, Annie Thomas asked me to lead a women's reading group on Charles Olson. The Gloucester Writers Center had recently acquired the Maud / Olson Library and we were trying to figure out how to make the library (and Olson) more accessible to our community.

At first I said yes. I have a habit of deciding to do a thing then figuring out how to do it. I hadn't read Olson since I was living in an apartment behind the Sawyer Free Library, before I was even legal to drink. I had served a brief stint as president of the United States branch of the Charles Olson Society, during which I was expected to serve as a sort of secretary across the border for Ralph Maud. I am not a good assistant and was not well suited to be treated as such by a man so many miles away.

After some thought I realized I wasn't ready to lead a group of women through Olson until I had made my own path through the Maximus poems.

Growing up in Gloucester, Charles Olson loomed over me as a writer. We walked the same streets, albeit years apart. My grandfather was his son's pediatrician. My friends, most notably Gerrit Lansing and Peter Anastas, were his friends. Still there was something keeping me from reading his work.

One Wednesday afternoon I decided it was time. I had just finished leading my writing groups at the GWC and had a couple hours before I had to get my children. I pulled a copy of the Maximus poems off the shelf and started.

My plan was to read a poem then write a reaction. I hoped that in doing so I would be able to draw some lines around Olson's

Gloucester and my own. Our paths would cross, but would he even see me on this island of men and girls?

I didn't know it, but I have a lot to say to Charles Olson. My reactions have become personal, a sort of conversation between me and Olson. They are, just as Maximus was, shaped by what is happening in our world, in our city, in our eyes. These poems are written after mass shootings, around protests and the Me Too movement. These poems are written as I raise my children.

This is not fun work but it feels important, and is best done with a deadline, most often a reading. The first poems in the series were published in the fourth issue of Joseph Torra's Let the Bucket Down. They can also be heard in the Gloucester Writers Center's media archives as part of the Speaking of Olson podcast in 2018.

I have a long way to go. Charles Olson took twenty years to write the Maximus poems. I still have some time.

Amanda Cook

Letter 6

I walked away from this for a long time.
I come back angry.

It's not that I think you are the problem. I can't separate you from
the problem.

I can't write this unless I am alone. Do you know how hard it is to
be alone these days?

Years ago my brother spent his nights sleeping on the deck of an
open boat, alone, out at sea, waiting to catch a tuna. One night he
showed up with a block of meat, bloody and red, from just behind
the fish's head. The rest he sold at auction. Does he have polis in
his eyes? He never had any money to pour back into his boat. He
raises his family in a small house looking over the city from the
edge of Dogtown.

Yesterday we went to a rally on the grounds of the meetinghouse
on Middle Street. A young girl stood, waiting her turn, as old white
men walked with determination to the front of the rally and took
the microphone before her. Do they have polis in their eyes?

Eyes,
& polis,
fishermen,
& poets

Maud talking to my bosom.
If he had looked up
would he have seen polis in my eyes?

Letter 7

This carpenter, who saw the tansy,
how could he have been the first?
The first to see tansy take root?

Gerrit's told me, gently, that I am not so right about tansy.
Not wrong, maybe, but not so right.

I expect whomever was here
watching tansy take root
before the carpenter arrived
knew how to use it.

1.

This carpenter,
who made things out of wood,
and who owned the land of the Cut,
and Al Gorman,
who kept sugar from his sister,
and Mason Andrews,
are they the cracks? The seams?
This commerce, this making and displaying,
this keeping sugar from one's sister,
this is American savage.

2.

I have a photograph of my mother at Whale's Jaw.
She is a child.
She looks not like she has conquered it,
rather like she is visiting an old friend.
Her siblings hang from the trees around her.
Whale's Jaw is broken now, cracked.

Some man or other made a fire beneath her
and she split.
I heard his name once, the man who broke her.
I did not remember it, nor was I surprised.

3.

My hands are short, stubby.
Peasant hands. Hands made for work.
My mother's hands were small, covered in paint.
Before she painted she worked with cloth.
Her hands too refused woman's flesh.

Tyrian Businesses

I'm not sure how I am supposed to feel about this poem.
I can tell you this: I don't feel good.

You say
there can be no more names
then there are objects
yet I am called
many things:

mother
wife
woman
daughter
goddess
slut
vessel

Letter 9

1

This year my garden is a mess.
My writing is a mess.
My art is a mess.
Nothing stops for any of it.
I have plums on my table.
A bowl of tomatoes.
A melon.
A glass of coriander, seeds heavy on thin stems.
An ambulance just passed on Washington Street.
The air feels like rain.

2

I could stay at my kitchen table.

I will, tonight.
My friends will come and our children will scatter to the
                        far corners of the house.
Someone might eat a plum. Light a candle.
We might close the windows as the air cools.
But tomorrow
I will rise early and stand up
against the whiteness and the fylfot.
Fuck the plum.

3

Starting in Roxbury,
watching the architecture change
which bricks they use, which greens,
which screens stay torn,

which windows hang which flags.
The differences of whitenesses.
The differences of blacknesses.
Trying to take up as little space,
as little breath.

Sometimes you leave the words to someone else.
Sometimes it's not your story to tell.

4

There is a buzzing around me.
Around everything around me.
I can feel it in my bones.

Above us
the helicopters
can't hear
our singing.

Letter 10

Cod or god,
power or power.
Let's not fool ourselves into thinking
either is sacred.

1

At a restaurant downtown
they have a drink named the Surinam Sling.
The Cape Ann Museum
tore down
the Pearce-Haskell House
without noting its ties to the slave trade.

Those great houses
lining Middle Street,
those captains weren't dealing in fish.

2
(there is no 2 in this poem, but in the middle of writing mine I have folded
three loads of laundry and peeled a tootsie roll off of the living room floor)

3

When I leave my city
and come back again
I am struck by how different Gloucester is.
How separate.
There is a danger in idealizing it.

Just last week
a drunk stumbled down Rogers Street
in a shirt marked

Black Lives Don't Matter.

4

Salem's a simulacrum.
In that game, the holding out,
we have won.
We keep our sins
neatly swept under the rug
and don't offer
tours on the hour.

Maximus, to Gloucester, Letter 11

(in which I swing from angry to sentimental)

That rock--
I once looked over
and saw my daughter, not yet ten,
climbing the face of that great rock.
I didn't yell
for fear of startling her.

I spent my childhood
climbing that rock, but the gentler slope,
and most often the stairs
carved out of the back.

I have called the DPW
to have a bench placed
at Stage Fort Park
to mark my father's life.
He is buried in West Gloucester,
by the marsh past Bond Hill.
My mother won't die, can't die.
I could get a bench for her anyway.

1.

Tragabigzanda.
Our own magic word, our secret history,
the street sign all the kids stole
until some man came from out of town
and tried to give us our own history
wrapped up in song and dance.
He used that name

As a password.
Stole it, took the cool right out of it.

2.

(in which my anger returns)

It is a difference in values, I suppose.
Those of us that make note
of what we feed the sick and dying.
That care, that care-taking,
Is another kind of attention.

3.

We cut it close.
Close, closed, we close off.
I have a fierceness in me
I let out
if someone I love is hurt.
I inherited this from my grandmother,
who would mutter Goddammit under her breath
as she walked around the house.
You, Captain (can I call you Captain?)
You have navigated into my waters.

Maximus, to Himself

I have made my life out of the simplest things.

A cup of coffee, a ball of yarn,
a simple song sung under my breath.

My life is full of ideas:
Laundry baskets, dirty dishes in the sink,
a jar of wilting roses.

I can almost imagine you standing
saying your words as I stand
holding a basket of clean clothes
against my hip,
waiting to be dismissed.

This morning the air was so cold
the harbor was full of sea smoke.
It rose around Ten Pound Island,
meeting the clouds that hung
at the horizon.
I drove home knowing
there was hot coffee in the pot.

The Song and Dance Of

See, that's just what I mean.
I would be standing for hours
waiting to fold the laundry.

Everybody knows tomatoes taste better
when you grow them yourself.

I am sure some man will tell me I am wrong.
Tell me I am doing it wrong.
To the left and to the right and to the center–
I want to bring all of them flowers.
To the president and his winning, I want to throw flowers at him.
 Cover him. Bury him in flowers, until he is lost in fragrance and
thorns.
I want there to be something to feel, some life, some love.

I want a bowl of oranges. A green glass bowl. But a man has
thrown away the green glass bowl. And the orbitron. And the rugs,
with all of their patterns and magic. Taken them out. These things,
this beauty, these bits of magic pose a risk.

I want a simple melody
Played on a piano
in one end of a long room
while the orbitron whirs.

Maximus, to Gloucester, Letter 14

I should tell you I don't really want to be doing this.
I am tired of your sash-weights, your man-men, and your names.
Mostly I am just tired.

The great men are naked. They are losing their crowns.

Everything about this, everything
feels like it should be left behind.
Except for the children.
Suck your gums, old man,
The children have had enough.

Maximus, to Gloucester, Letter 15

Some sons talk about their fathers.
Some sons keep quiet.

Sometimes all we are left
Are stories to reconstruct.

1.

It is a gift, knowing when to be quiet,
when to use your voice.

2.

There is broken glass
at the base of Tablet Rock.
I listen for the children
as they climb, no,
run,
up the side.
A tree grows
from the split in the rock.

I used to tell the kids
to be careful.

I don't bother anymore.

3.

I am skipping III.
Keeping quiet,
as it were.

4.

Some of us
have worked
the whole time.

Letter 16

We have more, I hope,
than how we make money.
More than our things.
We are more than we make.

1.

We can talk about what it means to lead.
What it means to be a leader.
We can talk about money and trusts
and we can talk about pejorocracies.
We would be talking, I think,
About men. At least now
when we have dismissed a woman
for being too sly
and put in her place
a fool, ready to
make America great.

How do we find good men?
How do we make them?
How can we keep men good?
They spoil so quickly.

The rocks from Cressy's beach
are all over the grass.
The man-made wall
couldn't hold back the storm.

2.

This country – this country!

Motherfucker.
They have pulled the rug
from under our feet.

3.

Hush.
We are talking back.

Maximus, to Gloucester, Letter 15 (revisited)

I would be lying if I told you I started this with an open mind.
Maybe that's not right. Maybe it was open,
but it was set, set on something in particular,
even if I couldn't name it.
There are bits of you, of your story, that you had no hand in.
I am sure this is true for all of us.

There are noises coming from every room in my house. I am going
to pour another cup of coffee and make a Manhattan and hope that
it will help me continue.

1.

I haven't written in some time. I haven't.
I haven't told you Gerrit died.

There. There it is.

I don't know why I held this, but I couldn't write more until I told
you.
Like I can't listen to my messages anymore. I haven't listened since
the week after he died.
Why bother? What am I going to hear?

I don't know that I will ever listen again.

2.

Smyth and Standish.
Standish and Smyth.

I have been rudderless for months. I don't want another navigator.
I want a chart, a sextant, a clear sky.

I wonder what I want to be.
The thing I keep coming to:
    I want to be
    quiet.

The seas were calm. The wind was fair
That made me so secure.

I am leaving time to grieve. I don't need, I don't want
to rush into some harbor. I have nothing in my hold, nothing to sell
onshore.
I am hollow. My ribs creak and ache with the waves.

That beacon above the harbor? That beacon is gone.

I have a piece of glass
stuck in my foot.
There is no tool better for finding broken glass
than bare skin.
I don't mind.
It reminds me that things break. People break.

I break.

3.

I don't know what to make of it. What comes of it.
I have the broom Gerrit gave me
when we bought our house.
When that broom is out of straw
I don't know what I will do.
I can't stop sweeping, although the floor looks like I have.
I will finish my coffee
and my Manhattan
and I will sweep the floor.

4.

O poets. You poets.

(I want to say something about tenderness, about talking to Annie
and Hettie and about Dale's talk about your letters with Duncan.
This may not be the poem for it, but I want to say it now, in case I
can't find the tenderness later.)

I am tender now. Sore, even.

Poets, let yourselves, let each other
be tender.

On First Looking Out Through Juan de la Cosa's Eyes

1.

Rough seas.
See–
Before we have a mappemunde
we still have our feet
on the ground.

2.

And the gods willed
he could leave her.
So it has been. So it shall be.
Slide into port,
set an anchor.

And whore–

3.

Fishy business, this Terra Nova.

I am not saying
anything new.
This discovery, this conquest–
this hard-gale land–
we tie it to the names of men.
I think of Tragabigzanda.

4.

Is she an apple,
a pear?

What shape
do her nipples take?
Respect her.
She lost her pearls
to a worm.

5.

The families
who can afford
Bouquets
needn't send their men
in ships
chasing cod.

6.

You have   no monopoly
          on the truth.

The Twist

This poem is a punch
to the gut.

The lines may as well be my trolley tracks.
I have been spending time in my past,
in my memory.

You have drawn lines back to all of it.
Back to my first house in Annisquam.
Back to the water.

These lines have the beauty of a storm coming in,
before the destruction.

1.

My first house in Annisquam was the smallest in the village.

My only memory there is my sister falling down the stairs. We
moved when I was three.

The resident before the current owners died in the house, and
nobody found the body for some time. I have heard the smell
described.

The memory of that smell recalled is stronger than my memory of
the house.

2.

Going through a box of my mother's fabric I found
a thick hook and eye, steel, each with an end threaded
to screw into wood

and I remembered my mother
locking me in my room,
the room next to hers,
so she and her lover could make love uninterrupted.

I remember hiding under a pile of blankets, listening
to the screaming and the banging, afraid.

When I was older and knew what the noises were I discovered
I could push a chair over and lift the hook out of the eye
with a baseball card slipped through the crack
and slip away, unnoticed.

3.

We share a history in these places.

I have been running from my childhood– no, walking,
briskly, keeping just a few steps ahead of it.
Crossing the cut as a child, and now, and again,
remembering the way a foot falls on a particular path to the sea.
I have the papers of my childhood. The places.

I have my children.

We are tied to the same places.
We know where the blackberries bloom.

Maximus, to Gloucester, Letter 19 (A Pastoral Letter)

1.

Teaching writing at McPherson Park. An old woman tells the story
of the deacon who drove her to Lynn to see her mother in the
nursing home.

At his funeral
his wife said
      some unpleasant things.

He was an alcoholic
      she said.

The old woman
      thought it wasn't polite
      to say.

I don't think it's nice,
      she said, and wondered
      if I agreed.

2.

Sunday mornings
we wake slowly
to the coo of the
mourning dove.
My daughter turns
her face
to the sun.

Letter 20: Not A Pastoral Letter

1.

how your own child awakes
how you have slumbered)

Last night too little, and lately too well,
waking with the first sounds of the birds through the open window,
      then staying, waiting, until my children climb in with me,
then soundly again with the sound of their breathing.

My mother died between that last poem and this.
I am avoiding a lot of things.
                    I can't avoid that.

She worked in fabric, my mother.
I have a studio full of her fabric.

By her death
she had lost
every bit of herself,
save her body.

2.

This poem is a standoff.

You have polis in your eyes.
Mine are wet with kaiho.

I carry your book like a weight
To bars, to work, to soccer practice.

It takes so long   to make the next poem.
This is
even as I carry your tome
      my poem.

3.

When my stepfather cleaned out my childhood home he had his
workers put so many of her things (our things) on the side of the
road. A neighbor let me know. Between the lunch shift and dinner
shift I was working I drove to Lanesville, filled my car, and emptied
it into my house three times. This was years before my mother
died. He sold the house to a fish smoker named Sasquatch. I don't
think it was his to sell.

4.

Our childhood was spent
fishing for change.
My mother was just starting to have money
when she started losing her mind.

I have a change purse, and another, filled with quarters
and a ten dollar bill. "I'll treat" she would say,
pulling out a change purse
as I slipped the waitress my money.

5.

Men who keep pawns.

(I could end this here, if I thought
the men who keep pawns
or use pawns
or play that particular game with people

would (could) see themselves in it)

In the annotated edition of this poem I will make note of my body.
Of the way men keep women.
Of the way my mother was kept
          alive   for years
and how the man who kept her
had the authority to do so.

6.

He is (you are)
a model   of a certain kind
          of success.

II

I am trying   these days
          to make do   with less.

My life is full of hand-me-down splendor.

I could show you where the best blueberries in Dogtown grow.

I will keep it to myself.

1.

I stand up straight
like my back
is against the wall.

POEMS BY JOHN MULROONEY / *Introduction*

John Mulrooney is a poet, teacher, musician, filmmaker, and archivist with a documentarian's sensibility. In this collection of poems, set in the cultural-political landscape of the U.S. under the regime of Donald Trump, we find a poet attempting to create order in a world on the brink of collapse. Within these poems is the desperate search for something to grasp onto, only finding "the occasional, the elliptical, the scattered / that of which I cannot speak / which is nevertheless what I remember." Nevertheless, Mulrooney digs deep into the chaos, untethering himself from time, place, history, mood, consciousness, leaving us untethered as well, but trusting and curious enough to come with.

Mulrooney shepherds us through history as we meet the ghost of a Harvard economist and ghosts of Confederate soldiers that lead us along the Natchez Trace. There are cracked cars and abandoned ships. A man in a flat black hat "comes along to tell us all that the world is one thing / and there is no way to make it any other." It is unnerving. It is bleak. We have stumbled into an eerily familiar darkness. It is 2019 in the United States, after all, a world of "motion of matter / departicularizing / into the indiscernible / a smashing of idols / a filtering of photons / a heraclitean stream of bullets." Even little Barron Trump wishes he were dead.

We time travel to the Civil War, the day of Liu Xiabo's death, Occupy Wall Street; from U.S. to China, Ireland to Senegal, Boston to Nashville, Shanghai to Gloucester. He writes, "I was from where I was from / until I was from somewhere else." In a time full of check-points, walls and cages, the poet is free to roam, to ask, "what we might do / when we aren't / seeking credit for / merely becoming awake."

Amongst all of the hallucinatory poetics are poems deeply rooted in

Mulrooney's lived experience. Having known John for many years, I would be remiss not to mention that he is one of the most active members of the creative communities he is a part of. Many of the poems are for or in conversation with his poetic comrades. His presence as a listener, organizer, and documentarian of the places that artists, poets and musicians congregate informs all of his work. In the stunning "Lines Composed on Amtrak, After Hearing Gerrit is Gone," Mulrooney writes of the passing of the great poet and his dear friend Gerrit Lansing. We are transported, given a celestial respite with the ecstatic call to arms: "See the light, the other light is come to join your light. Another world illuminated." It is very worth trusting in Mulrooney as guide through the wreckage. The map may be tattered, but he has found one. We are not as lost as we once thought.

Audrey Mardovich

John Mulrooney

Entaglement at Solstice

in one city light
fades the light
is fading to reveal
the darkness on
the day that is
the longest day
and it's your last
chance to play
the chess master
who will beat you
in the time it takes
to divide an hour
for the second time
by sixty as Sumerians
did and so now so
do you divide the hour
into superior highly
composite numbers
and the tablet
and the eye are two
sides of a triangle
and the third side
is the shape of
a lightning bolt
seen at dusk
on the longest day
is the shape of
Coltrane's tenor
looming lashing
from the speakers
is the shape of a
decision to take

down the mobile
of the Girl before
her Mirror the
decision to become
entangled in the last
thing that was in
the room before you
moved in 3D display
faded with the sun
morning sun in that
room the face and
the reflected face
replicated on both
sides and strung out
across the chop-stick
sized level plain like
rabbits strung on a hunter's
line in one city the mobile
of the painting is thrown
away a print of which
hung in the apartment
in another city near
where the original
Girl before her Mirror
hung and that print then
moved to another city
near where the original
Girl before her Mirror
was painted a city
in which the light
shows us that we
are the imperfect
recollection of light
shadows that show

where light wished
to be but failed
on the longest day
the last light dapples
the bare shoulders
of the chess masters
that cannot cling
or wait to suss out
the queen's whim
in the time it takes
to divide an hour
for the second time
by sixty and on
the longest day
a girl wanders among
the masters with
the Girl before her
Mirror on her t-shirt
the day you threw away
a mobile you failed
to throw away
before or were unable
but did in the time
it takes to divide
the hour for the
second time by sixty
of a painting
you neither care
for nor hate and
on that day you
can peel a yellow
sticky from
a compact disc with
Impressions, Spiritual,

Brasilia scrawled on it
and something
unreadable in a hand
you recognize
as your own
a hand no longer
yours that made
cuneiform on a slip
shod yellow sticky
Brasilia is a fake capitol!
Brassieres of famous doll!
Brothers, Jerusalem is ours!
(or was that an artificial capital)
stuffed into an envelope
containing a goodbye note
that was carried from
a city that was increment
to a city that was avalanche
in a folder of postcards
New Orleans, Cairo
Caravaca (where I was
once the marquis)
and a picture of you
who are always making
something out of nothing
with the writer of
a different goodbye
note and a picture
of Sonny Sharrock
and Alice Coltrane
you can peel a yellow
stickie off a cd
the particles of glue
cascade in the air

like tufts of incense
from a thurible
the particles of glue
the visible and
the invisible too
the smallest particles
smaller than the bit
depth of the songs
Impressions, Spiritual,
Brasilia first assembled
at the Village Vanguard
as particles of sound
in a different increment
of the city where
they reassembled
on a CD when John
Coltrane loomed
and lashed from
the speakers in
the apartment where
the print of Girl before
her Mirror hung
in this city
the chess masters
pack up the plastic
boards because
it is getting dark
the pieces hard
to distinguish
each unrepeatable
set of human
foibles become
the seeming same
no longer parts

of a whole
their movement
unintelligible
their action spooky
the girl with
the Girl before
her Mirror on
her shirt
disintegrating
in the parting light
the particles of
which are like
so much of
your own life
scrawled into
something
unreadable
in a hand you
recognize is
no longer yours
the hand of a
person who could
not answer why
you cling to this
and not to that
or why we divide
the hour into sixty
and then again
for a second time
and not another number
and then again
for a second time
or why this city
on the longest day

cracked by perfect
lightning lets you
throw away
and crumble
the glue that
entangled you
both close up
and at a distance

True Account of Ghost of John Kenneth Galbraith

I'm rushing to save you
and arrive at the station
to find you gone, gone
already, my note withheld
or just unread, the locket lost
and it's all too late -
is exactly how Central Square feels
on a winter night
after the votes are counted
and everyone has gone home
for the holidays.
Umbrellas in the street –
corpses after the coup
where the only sound is
Neil Young's "On the Beach"
played loud from a renegade taxi
who won't join the queue.
Ambushed just before
the gates of the manor house,
the dossier discovered, deceived
from within our own ranks
is exactly what the rain says we are
and the rain is false
but we won't deny it,
a rain rife with the seduction
of indifference, the lust
to forget, forget
to give it all away and quite
A sky the color of elephants
where the moon pokes through
though black as jackboots at the edges
present and indistinct as memory
even in the darkness the

stretched sky seems almost as supple
a construction as the mind
that hall wherein we will be haunted.
The world is turning.
I don't wanna see it turn away.
Get in the cab.
and remember the cabbie
as the man who saw
the ghost of John Kenneth Galbraith
and yourself as the person he chose to tell,
or don't remember him as that –
not at first. First, be all diligence.
First, remember nothing,
then once out of the cab
when the body is stalled by
the rain's lies, the lying rain
of winter –
remember they were friends
and how Galbraith used
to talk about Lincoln
in the very seat you were in
and the rain lies
the skin breaks in a dry season
leaves seethe in the wind
you seem to move right through yourself
like we used to think ghosts did
you are a breeze on a full clothesline
you are air and you are what air does
to drying things
then remember they conversed
for an hour until the nurse
came in and Galbraith vanished
remember all of this after
he says he voted to make America
great again.

Now it is the chase scene
confederate ghosts lead hounds
along the Natchez Trace
paddyrollers holler and troll
as we try to make it to the sea
black mirror says this way
black mirror says that way
a Confederate ghost on TV
calls out race traitors and
the old industrial state
collapses everywhere in Union Square.
the ghost of Little Willie Lincoln
sings a lament to Colonel Edward Baker
his father's advisor and friend
fallen at Ball's Bluff
in October of '61 –
a full two years before the swamp angels
would march from Camp Meigs.
Keckley records Little Willie
was devoted to verse and mischief
and equally so to memorizing
train time tables
he knew that a poem is
a kind of schedule
he himself dead before
the spring rains would come,
typhoid in the white house water
drawn from the muddy Potomac
in which soldiers and horses
shat and dumped camp trash
his mother mary todd
saw him wandering in
the east wing
conversed with him
outloud and through mediums

he sang her songs she hummed back to him
the cabinet thought of committing her
the president sat in silent grief.
the congress conspired
that soothsayers ran the white house
and in this version our fingers
clutch the bony rocks that gird the cliffs
the bootsoles crush our knuckles
on top of president's heads.
Barron looks like
there's so much mischief
he wants to avoid
if he could disappear
like a typhoid stricken child
like the bodies unmarked
at Charleston and Bull Run
if he could only disappear
like a fact, teetering in a synapse
like the affluent society
a chart we no longer need
a timetable superseded
the appointment missed
the train gone from the station
the turning world, turning away.

A Short Mute History of Locusts and Cicadas

which is nevertheless what I remember
but I couldn't speak of it
the incident with the locusts

which I thought were cicadas
a riot of dark photons out of an alley
a fleet of winged shouting tongues

a swarm and then the slow replacing
of the swarm with something more,
thicker, stable and sluggish

if there was a word for this
you would form it by mouthing
'wonder' but hearing 'terror'

but I couldn't speak of it
the locusts rose from the ground
and scattered across the sky

and from behind a locust curtain
a world emerged that you could
almost swear was this one we are in.

the cicadas here are bigger than your fist
wrap around the sound of jackhammers
and the tolling of temple bells

on the day Liu Xiabo died
I sat in a coffee shop in Shanghai
learning to make the characters

of Mao Tse Tung's name

from a twenty year old girl
who sang Taylor Swift at karaoke

the word for rubbing two words/names together
has the sound of an extinct bird in it
and must be formed purely by luck

the best dumplings in Shanghai
can be ordered without speaking
a series of gestures, hands waving

in the sleepy clamor
of the French concession
on the day of the words fire and fury

unlike the world has ever seen
which must be formed by
trying to tear the wings off other words

the word for rolling your tongue over
a piece of food you wish was a word
a firm piece of comprehension

that tastes like truth is made
by stridulation of the spleen
and the lower intestine

the incident with the locusts
sent its shock through me
because all I know of pattern

is the occasional, the elliptical, the scattered
that of which I cannot speak
which is nevertheless what I remember

Merely

for Anselm Berrigan

it takes five minutes
to read two poems
called Jim Brodey
then the Braintree train
comes and there are still
three more poems called
Jim Brodey because
a year has past since
the emergency when
I lost a patron saint
of memory and the city's
sirens choired outside
my window while
for all four quarters
of the Super Bowl I lay
in my hospital bed
waiting for my sister
to come around again.
There will come a time when
I will look at the word
"singularity" and know
what it really means.
This will be before
or after the coming
of the singularity
and before or after
the city emerges as
a city where time
present and past
fight over who will
blame it on the coin toss

when they don't beat the spread
and in this time
the real less and less really
strange moods of silence
broken by the broken-hearted
breath of fare jumpers
assing through the cars
of a Braintree train
thrashing pigeon both
possum and chameleon
gray on gray tile
really pyrrhic pigeon
drop-kicked and clutched
by art or nature
camouflaged jiu-jitsued
feet and feathers all
a rage not silent
that wants to feel
fortified by the stability
of any invocation
what we might do
when we aren't
seeking credit for
merely becoming awake
or merely remembering
not to block a doorway
when you stand
at a terminal station
for five full minutes
gazing at an open field
and feel the moist fold of its leaves
through your eyes in the mere
of what merely really is

Pareidolia

faces in the hedgerows
appear in the late dusk
the muddy green darkens
reveals fluid smiles
placid anguishes
quivers of faces, hardly faces
the light lighting out
a question unanswered
a darkness revealed
the ruddy face of dusk
fading to the nothing burger
of darkness
darkness beneath the dusk
above the wreckage
of a pick-up truck at the mouth
of the abandoned village
and its wreckage that
has graduated to ruin
blank pedestals covered
in lichens and moss
the Noamhogs absent
smashed
with missionary zeal
as far as we can discern
a face in darkness is itself
darkness soon enough
a mouse in a humane trap
makes little plastic sounds
in a dusk that reveals
this day like any other
slipping into a different
like any other

John Mulrooney

a like any other
you thought you knew
the day you took
a different mouse
humanely to the landfill
as a benevolent god
the slate blue clouds
a panther with a third eye
a tray of figs and lemons
a nest of cobalt eggs
or ritual stones
a copse of trees
ready to burst
an explosion of starlings
seen from the shore
that mimic the quick motion
of steam up from the sink
that obfuscate the hedgerows
disappearing in the dusk
before both are forgotten
a motion of matter
departicularizing
into the undiscernible
a smashing of idols
a filtering out of photons
a hereclitean stream
of one shape saying no
and then many shapes
saying no, no, no
a day in which the shape
of another day fits
perfectly like a you-sized

disguise of you, your own face
covered by this face   59

a like any other you know
but haven't seen
like the faces in the hedgerows
you can no longer discern
a blank like any other
like the day
we went to that store
in the thawing snow
but that store was closed
the shafts of sunlight
finding their way beneath
the bridge the highway
that spanned the river
astonished the roofs and gutters
the whole day was
revealed as the day that
other days had only
been the placeholder for
so that even when we
went back out into the light
and the familiar territory
it was new - a familiarity
that had not happened
before.
Noamhog means ship
or god or maybe ship
and god or maybe godship
a magic that crosses water
no one knows that or
even if they guarded
the abandoned village
in the time before it was
abandoned but at least
there are songs about it

songs of smashed idols
that might just have been
cracked cars, or just
abandoned ships
that sing
I was from where I was from
until I was from somewhere else
I used to wear a smock
that was ever renewed
and came through near
the wreckage came
through the near wreckage
near came through
the wreckage came near
through the wreckage
it was all it was all
around me - the unseasonable
around me the music
it was all without measure
it was all occasionally it
made you feel empathy for
a creature perceived to be
weaker than oneself a
creature nearly come through
the wreckage but the
wreckage meant it could
no be measured the music
the mouse in the humane trap
who is the same mouse who was in
the humane trap before.
but looks different each time
or is a different mouse
who looks the same each time
like the school shooter just now

who looks like the school shooter then
the face that will stay
wanting to not stay
a shape that says no no no
forever in a heraclitean stream of bullets
he looks like the last like any other
you would see before becoming
the like any other
you never thought you'd be
if you don't take a mouse
over a body of water
or over a major highway
it will return home
as it were to what you call your
home or wherever you have
not abandoned yet
and so you really have
been taking the same
mouse to the abandoned landfill
if you won't cross the water
in the ship of whatever god
you wish to be
the doctor can't comment
on the ages of the victims
or the prognosis of the
wounded
the plain answerable questions
put on dumbshow to
keep us from the unanswerable
how it is that someday wreckage
graduates to ruin
the arms of the woman
gesticulating on the playground
obscure her face

John Mulrooney

hands open and close
like birds trapped in hedgerows
reach out touch the
human form not fully in the frame

that cannot be discerned
seeking a shape that will say yes

John Mulrooney

Pastoral Composed en Route to a Political Fundraiser

A purple finch blockades the sun where we
await the most instructive impossibilities.

We fondle money that is crisp like snow
and everything parades in front of us and then is gone.

In December, the philosophers can be seen
going for walks at the dump;

their harvest of leisure is your harvest too –
attack ads are what society thinks we do,

but our mothers know we are nice boys.
The season sweeps up with what seems like single mindedness,

playing its part, knowing its past, respectful of tradition
and drinking our skin into its cold silky mouth;

that soundproof cavern wherein we sing our Christmas song –
there's a pudding party somewhere but we can't find it,

there is a lavender house that magically turns purple.
And we'll never get back to where once inside

we built a bridge between revert and restore,
asked for sweets and received them –

the full roundness of our mouths only realized
by the joy we filled them with and once realized,

that joy, confirmed the joys we only dimly remembered –
a cold winter day softened by confectionary snowmen and angels;

a concession speech so gracious the victors would quote it with

John Mulrooney

But just then the man in the flat black hat and the umbrella

comes along to tell us all that the world is one thing
and there is no way to make it any other –

and the buds have all been fooled;
and the crunch of our feet in the snow,

the lattice work of winter trees,
our thoughts of Charles Darwin

and the voyage of the Beagle –
are all distractions that will destroy him.

The man in the flat black hat is crying
and only the candidates can hear.

They say someday that winter will end
and the birds will long to have somewhere to long for –

this crisp air that holds your cheeks only makes you think of
                                        another time,
the hint of crisp in the air is the first word of a poem of the snow,

the crunch of feet and the lattice work of winter trees will be a song
a purple finch will sing from the perch outside the feeder.

This hint of snow is a meme we will outgrow accordingly.

Poems on the Epiphany

for John Wieners

a gust of snow on Massachusetts
avenue plumes angelic
like chalk dust from erasers
that let you escape
a lie – wipe it
away and forget
it was ever meant for you.
This is how we acquaint grace –
not in a day, but little by little,
diminuation of belief in false gods
that never hear our prayer.
I will go and follow the snow
monkeys,
traverse distressed branches
to avoid the icy slopes,
until peat moss and fiddle heads –
scant slivers of spring
peek through –
revelation in the snow

John Mulrooney

Wallahi le Zein

for Filip with an F

today the ground is closer to the helicopters
dress it undress it our wound is now the chrysalis
of the peripheral greenery reformation

dress it undress it and it gives us something to do
so I shop - as I do - I am always shopping for
the newest Mauritanian psychedelia

and find it and recall - for all commerce is a kind
of recall - of recalling - the border village near
San Louis where I was blinded in both my eyes

but not blinded like I was at Toubab Diallo
but blinded by the sun and had to take someone's
word on how lucrative the fishing industry was

how the violent glint shimmered crepuscular
off scales waiting to be scraped and shucked and thrown away
such luxury of light and carp and mackeral

of light that cuts violently under the eyelids
reveals an inner light in silhouette – even more
how not like the light of searchlights above the city

that propel us into darkness at a thousand points
make us blanked and blinded deafened beneath propellers
but not like when we were blind in the blank of the sun

at the edge of Boston wailing for our demon lovers
or waiting for Corita's tank to screech across the sky
or sorrowful fumbling with our trembling actor hands

and woke at night with sweats and short breath like we used to
trying to recall all we could of risk management
recite the principia mathematica

bear in mind the special relationship we maintain
with the republic of sleight of hand – don't we all wish
we had benzedrine enough to carry us back there

but it's a long road and when you build a road you know
there will be fighting - when you build a wall you had best
already made your wreathes – the republic of thought knows

the faces of children crack and leak the refugees
of the next war and the strategic planning session
has been post-poned until we all agree that hunger

is not yet market ready and poverty may stain
wolfman say the blind spend the world the blind spend the world
and scatter vanished shadows upon us with no trace

you can detect - my demon lover is a photon
rising from Zucotti Park - I heart the republic
of the burning libraries of the sky arranging light

now it's dreamland America all over again.

John Mulrooney

Lines Composed on Amtrak, After Hearing Gerrit is Gone

A lone swans swans up the river at Old Saybrook,
    The last bit of snow slithers between fall and flurry.

Light rolls above our heads,
      stars and the reflection of stars,
          headlights and the reflection of headlights,
Merge in the glass.

And below
      The Quinebaug River gone pointillist
think crust of ice in the shallows,
some mud or other rage below the surface.

See the light, the other light
is come to join your light.
Another world illuminated.

Still it's hard to see
      night creeping in to Mystic.
Orange and yellow earth movers
a fading gleam in winter twilight –
Tonka trucks tearing up the soluble forest.

      You lie in state at stage fort park –
your voice the milk of stars
a passage opening in the thicket.
The earth's mouth a door to the infinite.
The route, the way,
          the map of the way.

THE SEARCH FOR PLEASURE WITHOUT LOVE: OVID'S CURES FOR LOVE

Ovid's "Love poems," *The Art of Love* and *The Cures for Love*, were immensely popular in their time and have exerted a wide influence on European civilization. Chaucer was not the only poet who read Ovid's love poems, so did almost every educated person with any interest in the subject. His wit and humor were often lost among medieval scholars who recast his themes in terms of "courtly love," an idea that would have seemed ridiculous to Ovid. His women are often "found on the street" and in one poem he speaks specifically of a "prostitute in Rome." He repeatedly speaks of love (i.e. sex) as a strategic game where the stakes are very high and the loser often suffers greatly. Thus Ovid, the poet, takes on the role of the doctor, providing "cures" for those who have contracted "love's virus." His previous work, *The Art of Love*, taught men how to seduce women and how to keep their lovers. His *Cures for Love*, on the other hand, teaches, primarily men, how to fall out of love; but to be fair Ovid writes,

But don't mistake me, girls, I am speaking to you as well as to the boys
I arm you both with these lessons in love
and if what I say doesn't directly concern you
don't worry, you may learn something anyway from the examples I provide.

The voice and subject matter of these poems are surprisingly modern. The poems are ironic, cynical, as times even satirical, and essentially promote a hedonistic lifestyle. I sometimes think of *The Cures for Love* as the first "self-help" book; it so frank in its advice and severe in its methods that future generations would find the book distasteful. In Lempriere's Classical Dictionary (1809) we find this amusing description of The *Cures for Love* and its companion volume: "...the doctrine which they hold forth is dangerous, and, as the composition of an experienced libertine and refined sensualist, they are to be read with caution, as they seem to be calculated to corrupt the heart, and sap the foundations of virtue and morality." Ovid tells lovers to avoid their partners in the hope of eventually becoming bored with them, not to use magic to ensnare the beloved as it will only backfire on the lover, to spy on their lover in the bathroom in order to see that their beauty is constructed with makeup and not real, and above all, to never to be jealous; finally, he advises the lover to have multiple partners to rid thoughts of the beloved from his mind.

Ovid is a realist disguised as an aesthete and vice versa. The beloved object is the subject of various projections on the part of the beloved. He sees her as a beautiful object. This is important to understand, otherwise Ovid's remedy concerning excessive behavior would not be believable. Greco-Roman ideas of the Beautiful have greatly influenced European culture. It is this classical idea of "beauty" that Ovid criticizes. He sees the naked body as if on the operating table. The world of appearances is debased in favor of reality, which is shocking to the lover, and causes the mirage of love to fade. On the other hand, the illusion of beauty and sensuality can also be destroyed in another way, through excess which breaks unconscious habits. Finally, for Ovid, it is best to "please yourself" and to have multiple sexual partners; and if you decide not to keep love totally out of the picture, then at least keep Cupid at bay. With this advice Ovid concludes The Cures for Love.

I imagine Ovid as a fiercely independent poet, willing to follow his own desires, despite resistance from his father. Here's another quote by John Lempriere, from his famous *Classical Dictionary:*

As he was intended for the bar, his father sent him early to Rome, and removed him to Athens in the 16th year of his age. The progress of Ovid in the study of eloquence was great, but the father's expectations were frustrated; his son was born a poet, and nothing could deter him from pursuing his natural inclination, though he was often reminded that Homer lived and died in the greatest poverty.

That he ended his life in exile, under mysterious circumstances, only confirms that his poetry must have carried a certain dangerous emotional current that ran counter to the Imperial era. It would also be a disruptive force in the centuries to come.

1

Love, I know you saw the cover of my new work and read *The
Cures for Love*
and said: "So you want to fight, you want a war, is that it?"
Cupid, don't accuse your poet of blasphemy. I'm innocent, I, who
often
held up the standard that you consigned to my care, and obeyed
your every wish.
I'm not Diomede, who wounded your mother, poor woman
whom Mars helped and returned to bright heaven on his wild
horses.
Other young men often temper their fires: but I've always loved,
and if you were to ask me what I'm doing at this moment,
I'd tell you, "Making love." And to prove it
I've taught your Art, as well, and how men can get into your good
graces,
and how suddenly overwhelming passion can surrender to reason.
Gentle Boy, I haven't rejected you but always faithfully taught your
Art,
and this new Muse who drives the pen in my hand now
will not disgrace your prior work.
Let any man who loves and is loved in return, rejoice and be happy
and delight in the ecstasy of love: let him sail with a favorable wind.
But any man who suffers wrongly from the witchcraft of some
devious bitch,
won't have to lose his life if he understands the essence of my Art.
Why should any lover tie a rope around his neck and hang himself
from the ceiling and die such a miserable death?
Why should anyone slit his own wrists with a cold knife?
You're the lover of peace, but you earn the people's hate for such
deaths.
If a man's life is in danger because he can think of no one else but
her then let him forget her as fast as he can:
and then, Cupid, you won't be responsible for the funeral.

And after all you're just a boy: not fit for this kind of trouble but for
play and games:
So play then: at your age it's not right to think of battle.
For you might have used your arrows to make war:
but I see they're not tinged with blood.
Of course, your stepfather Mars is another story,
picking fights with swords and sharp spears,
and when he's victorious he struts on the battlefield amid all the
blood and gore:
but you're a mamma's boy, and not fit for such recklessness,
except, of course, if your mother Venus impels you to act,
at least here they'll be no risk of broken ribs or legs
and no parent will shed tears for the loss of her son.
You cause some doors to break off their hinges, as men fight over
love,
while pretty wreaths hang from others.
You cause a young man and a shy girl to meet and fall in love
and cheat the foolish husband with elaborate tricks.
And then you let the lover who had the door shut in his face, flatter
her
and then he curses the damn door, and then he weeps, then he
sings to her.
Be content at least that these are only tears,
and that you don't have another death on your hands:
but it's not right for your torch to stoke the burning pyres.
So I spoke: golden Love turned the ring on his middle finger,
and said to me: "Continue the work as planned."
So listen to my words you young men who've been deceived,
you who have utterly been betrayed by the one you love.
Learn the secret cure from I, who first initiated you into the art of
love:
the hand that wounded now will cure.
In Nature there are herbs that heal and those that harm,
and the thorn is never far from the rose:
The same spear with which Achilles pierced his enemy, Telephus,

was then able to heal him.
But don't get me wrong, girls, I'll tell you everything I tell the men.
I'll arm you both against Love:
and if you find that my words don't apply to you directly,
you can still learn all you need to know by example.
It's always a good idea to put out a wild fire,
don't let your heart be enslaved by your failed relationships.
Phyllis went to the shore nine times to wait for her husband's return
but it was one time too many, and depressed, she killed herself.
Dido would not have witnessed Aeneas' fleet
departing from the shore, nor cursed him and the Trojans
as she fell upon a sword on the pyre built for her.
Nor would Medea have been filled with such rage against her husband
that she murdered her own children in an act of revenge.
By becoming an adept in my art,
Tereus would not have been so consumed with lust
that he raped Philomena and cut her tongue out to keep her silent
nor would he have been transformed into a bird for his crime.
Hand Pasiphae over to me, and her love for the bull would have disappeared.
And Phaedra? Her shameful love for Hippoylytus likewise would have vanished.
Entrust Paris into my care and Menelaus would have had his Helen,
and Troy would not have been vanquished by the Greeks.
If impious Scylla had only read my verses
she would not have fallen in love with Minos,
nor stolen the purple lock from her father Nisus,
which made him invincible.
With me at the helm, you can dry your tears,
my ship and crew will sail freely over the windswept waves.
Look, you can see the glistening shore from here.
You've read your Ovid before on the subject of love

now read this, Ovid's newest book, and understand love's other
face.
I call on the public and ask them to hear me.
I loosen the shackles that hold you bound to a master.
My words may seem harsh to some
but you must praise the whip that gives you freedom from pain.
Apollo, god of medicine and song,
may your laurel guide me, I beg you, as I begin
these harsh lessons of love.
You bring relief to doctor and poet alike,
in the grips of hopeless passion,
and both can benefit from your wisdom and care.

2

If you don't really want to be there and your feelings are lukewarm,
then stop, while you still can, and don't ring that bell.
Crush the first stirrings of illness before you get an infection,
and don't let your horse take another step
until you're sure you're moving in the right direction.
The passage of time strengthens reserve.
Time ripens the grape and adds to its taste,
and produces firm healthy crops
from young tender shoots.
The tall tree that provides shade for the wanderer
was once a small seed that first had to be planted,
and that could be pulled from the soil with ease,
but now, fully grown, it stands immovable with its roots deep in the
earth.
Be absolutely certain of who you love,
and withdraw your neck from the irksome collar or it will begin to
itch.
Stop the progress of the disease from the beginning.
If the tumor continues to grow no doctor will be able to operate.
Hurry! Don't just wait around.

Don't procrastinate or it'll be too late tomorrow to resist:
Love is full of traps and gains in strength while you wait,
while you put off for later what you could do today.
The best day to begin is any day,
and soon you'll be on the road to freedom.
Single rivers are never very broad at their origin:
it's the many smaller rivers that merge to create a vast sea.
Myrrha, if you hadn't tricked your father into having sex with you,
you would not have been transformed into the tree that bears your
name.
I've seen a tumor become cancerous
if not treated at once and the patient suffer miserably.
But since we're fascinated with the charms of Venus,
we always say: "Maybe tomorrow will be different."
Meanwhile, the fire burns in our heart,
and the Tree of Grief drives its roots deeper.
But if that first chance to snap it in the bud is lost
and that old feeling begins to rise again in the heart,
the greater the work that needs to be done: but because I've been
called
to treat the disease at a later date, don't think I'll abandon the
patient
and pronounce him a lost cause and as good as dead.
That part of Philoctetes' foot that was wounded and became
infected
could have caused his entire foot to be amputated:
but they say, having been healed, that many years later
he was the one who dealt the final blow that ended the Trojan war.
I, who worked under pressure to catch the virus in its early stages,
now at last, can speak to you calmly about relief from pain.
You must either quench a fire when you smell smoke,
or when it has died down, having exhausted its fury.
If you're both on fire then wait for it to pass:
all of us would find approaching a blazing fire a bit tricky.
No swimmer in his right mind would go against the current,

if he could swim to the other side and reach the shore.
Of course, the restless spirit, that has no traction, hates my art,
and won't listen to my advice.
But I'd better have a word with him now.
Since the wound is fresh he'll be more likely to listen.
Only a lunatic would tell a mother to stop weeping at the death of
her child,
because she is in no position to listen to his words.
But when tears have stopped and the spirit of sadness is exhausted,
then grief can find words to express itself.
The remedy must be applied at the right time:
wine can help, but at other times it can lead to terrible confusion.
Now if you try to deny it, you may even provoke and aggravate the
disease.
Remember, my Art requires precision.
So when you're ready to take the cure,
listen to me: don't be idle, do something.
When you have nothing to do
thoughts of love start to preoccupy your mind
and you encourage this because you feel good.
Know then that love shares the same bed with evil.
If you're occupied with work, Cupid slams his darts to the ground,
frustrated,
his bright torch is extinguished and everyone curses him.
Now some people are drawn to the arts, some to finance,
and still others enjoy sports,
but Venus loves a man who has nothing to do.
If you want love to leave you alone,
occupy yourself with some work:
keep busy and love will stay out of your way.
If you never get out of bed and are always bored
and if you gamble away everything you earn
and spend too much time in the bars
you'll be weakened, sure, but your heart will still be pumping:
Love is patient and strikes when you're not looking.

That blind Boy just sits around doing nothing: he hates the hard
worker.
Here's an exercise: give your empty head something to think about.
You could study Law, become a Supreme Court Judge and learn to
defend your friends.
Then you'll associate with the intellectual crowd in Rome.
Or you could join the military and serve battle-hungry Mars:
then I'm sure you won't have love on your mind.
Look, the Parthian is running away, this proves Caesar is
victorious,
his men have totally occupied the enemy territory:
Vanquish both Cupid and Parthia and break their spears
and bring back a trophy to your native gods.
Diomede, favorite of Zeus, wounded Aphrodite
and in response to his transgression,
she ordered her lover to fight on her behalf.
You ask why Aegisthus seduced Clytemnestra, Agamemnon's wife.
The answer's clear: he was bored and couldn't think of anything to
do.
All the mighty Greeks were eager to fight and rushed to the
battlefield.
"Slaughter the Trojans" was their motto.
If he felt like stirring up some trouble with local punks,
he couldn't. No one was around.
If he wanted to argue in the Courts of Argos, there were no
lawsuits!
There was nothing to do and so he made love.
My sweet Boy, this is how you find a way into our hearts.

5

If for some reason you need to stay in the City,
(Ah, let me guess: your mistress!), then please listen to my advice
from the City.
That man who snaps the chain around his heart frees himself from

pain
and he won't have to feel sorry for himself anymore.
But this man's a special case to marvel at and I do
and say to myself: "Here's someone who won't have to fear my
predictions."
It's for you, who can't stop loving or forgetting past mistakes
but who desperately want to, and always fail, for you I am writing
this book.
Recall every wicked thing your girl has done,
and remember all the hurt she's caused you.
"I give her everything she desires, but she's never satisfied with
anything:
she's such a greedy wench that even the household gods gave
notice the other day.
She swore to me that she was pure and innocent, and, I, the fool,
believed her
waiting for hours at her door, until I could barely stand up!
She treats all her lovers with kindness and values their company
but spits on me when I say I love her and wants nothing to do with
me,
a drug dealer has nights with her, but I get the cold shoulder!"
Let all this corrupt your feelings:
as you remember, discover the origin of your hatred.
Ask yourself how you could have loved her!
Suffer until you can't take it: the more you suffer
the more eloquent the expression of your suffering will be.
Recently I was attached to a girl I met in Rome
but she didn't seem to be interested:
Like a modern day Podalirius I tried to cure myself with drugs and
alcohol
but I was not like him and couldn't cure myself that way.
I felt better when I contemplated the defects of her body:
"How ugly her legs are" I'd say to myself
and yet they were very pretty.
"How her arms sag" I'd say to myself

and yet they really didn't.
'How short she is!' but she wasn't
"After I went broke trying to support her expensive habits
she asked me for money to buy larger jewels"
And that's where I draw the line.
I hated her most for that reason.
The good is so close to the bad
we often mistake one for the other.
Develop a habit mocking your lover
and purposely warp your judgment.
Confuse the boundary between good and bad:
Call her "manly" if she has an athletic build.
If she's "dark skinned" call her black.
If she's thin say she looks like a "skeleton."
If she's modest, call her a "brazen whore."
If she's honest, say she's "gullible."
Encourage those talents your woman lacks,
and applaud her great efforts:
If she can't sing have her practice Rosina's part in the score from
Rossini's opera.
If she can't dance to save her life audition her for the Russian
ballet.
If she speaks like a barbarian let her recite Proust.
If she can't play a single chord ask her play a fugue on the guitar.
If she develops asthma when she runs sign her up for a marathon.
If she has pimples on her breast spend a lot of time at a topless
beach.
If her teeth are ugly learn as many jokes as you can to make her
laugh.
If she has watery eyes tell her stories that make her cry.
And if you can, surprise her at dawn
when she has no make-up on her face.
She'll put on a fancy dress, wear jewelry and look great,
so we don't think of her imperfections,
but what we see is not the truth about her.

Ask yourself: where's that special thing I love about her
behind all those gems and fancy dresses.
All this "putting on of appearances" deceives the lover.
Surprise her when she's not expecting it
and you'll find all her faults in plain view.
That should be enough to devalue her in your eyes.
But, unfortunately, this is not always the case.
Sometimes "the fresh, natural look" is deceptive.
Finally, what you must do is spy on her
while she's applying all that make-up in front of the mirror.
You'll see her mix all the colors of the rainbow,
and various other concoctions, some of which drip onto her sagging
tits.
She does this to achieve an effect.
But the whole bathroom stinks like Phineus' dinner table
and recalling that stench even now makes me want to vomit.

6

Now comes the subject you've been waiting for: SEX.
And I will again speak clearly and say,
"Love has no place in a discussion of sexual matters."
You might be saying to yourself, "Ovid, now you have gone too far
in separating love from sex."
O man of little faith! Stay with me as I continue to unravel my
theme.
The censors will have my ass if I don't watch out
but even if I hold back a little you'll get what I'm trying to say.
You must understand that I've already been put on trial for the
contents of my books
and my Muse has been called "filthy-mouthed" by the puritan
critics.
But they can drag me and my Muse through the mud all they want,
my books continue to sell and are read throughout the world.
Zoilus, a renowned critic in his time, wrote a negative review of

Homer's book.
No one remembers this critic now but Homer's genius is
recognized by all.
Poor Virgil, these same critics tore apart your book in an issue of
the New Yorker,
you who brought the customs and gods of Troy back to Rome.
Slander always seeks to devalue great writing
just like the winds that hurl themselves onto the peaks of
mountains
and yet, like Jove's thunderbolt, the Truth comes crashing down on
the critic's bald head.
But you who persist in thinking my poems deal with offensive
subjects
and are just trash fit for the garbage dump.
Please reconsider everything in its proper context.
Homer's verse deals with men at war and there is no place for love
here.
Tragedy strikes a sublime note and noble rage is tragic,
and comedy is derived from the public sphere.
The poetic line can go wherever it will, gathering speed or slowing
down,
or launching into a full out attack on the enemy.
An elegiac poem satisfies Cupid who readies his arrow to tug at the
heartstrings.
Elegia is a gentle mistress urging us to remember the dead
in ways she finds appropriate.
There is no place in Callimachus' verse for the anger of Achilles.
Homer's voice is not suitable to sing of the sweetness of Cydippe.
Could you imagine Thais playing the part of Andromache?
Even if she tried, the audience would cringe and the theater would
quickly empty.
But the playfulness of Thais suits my Art and if my Muse is ok with
that
then the charges brought against me will be thrown out of court
and I'll be released, a free man again.

So, sickly-faced Envy, drop dead! The name "Ovid" is known
throughout the world and if I am allowed to continue elucidating
my theme,
then Fame will surely secure a position for me among the greatest
poets of all time.
Be patient, don't leave my group if you know what's good for you
because my mind is on fire and this is only the 6th poem of my
projected work.
My desire for glory increases with each newly completed poem
and I feel that there must be a god on my side.
The wild stallion I ride upon is eager to climb the highest
mountain.
Elegia tells me in confidence that she owes as much to me
as her brother, The Epic, owes to Virgil.
Tell this to Envy and watch the bitch squirm.
Now Ovid, go your own way, until you reach the end of your theme,
confident in the power of each line.
Listen: if you've waited all night and your nuts are swelling up,
don't just rush over to your mistress and waste all your juice on her
but find another and let her extract some of the milk.
Remember, it won't be as intense the second time around
but sweeter than having to wait all night for it.
When it's cold outside we wish for the summer heat.
In summer we seek the shade. And if we're thirsty a tall glass of
water hits the spot.
I shouldn't say it but I will anyway: When you're having sex with
your mistress
take her in a position that's least flattering to Love. Say, from
behind.
I'm sure this won't be a problem. Women are essentially perverse
creatures.
They don't like to admit the truth about themselves.
They would like us to think that every aspect of their body is
beautiful.
Open the windows when you're having sex and see her body in

broad daylight.

Notice the countless imperfections of the skin: pimples, rashes, swelling, stretch marks.

Now when it's over and your exhausted and lying in bed, regretting that you ever touched a woman in the first place, and vowing never again to do so for a long time, then just think of all these defects in her beauty and remember them.

When you get home add them to your list.

Ok, ok I know what you're thinking: "beauty is only skin deep." But you're armed with your list.

And the more you add to it the greater the effect will be.

The bite of a snake can kill a bull, and a wild boar is often silenced by a rather small hound.

Know that my methods are numerous.

There are so many "ways" of doing things, so many "positions," I don't think I have to give them all.

A joke that's funny to one person will outrage another, so too, if I were more explicit I would anger all those "tight-lipped" conservatives.

A man who was turned on by seeing his woman in a new dress might go limp when he sees her naked. Thus the raging fire is quenched.

Another man, after he's done having sex with his woman, feels the wet bedspread under his ass and is revolted by love's excretions.

I know you still might be having doubts about my methodology.

You'll say, "If he really loved her he wouldn't bother about any of this."

But wait until that Blind Boy starts shooting his darts at you and then you'll change your tune.

You'll suffer and find yourself wishing that you had listened to that poet, Ovid.

Now how about that man who secretly looks into the bathroom and see what his woman does from the moment she wakes up,

and becomes sick to his stomach?
Now the gods tell me not to suggest such things, and even threaten
to take me to court,
saying the modesty of a woman should be respected.
For this reason I wouldn't trust the gods
to give sound advice when speaking of the reality of love.

10

Near the Collinian gate there is a sacred shrine
that gets its name from the Venusian mountain Eryx.
The deity who reigns there is called Oblivion.
It he who gives aid to the sick at heart
by dipping Love's torch into the cold waters of Lethe.
It is here that young men come to forget their trials in love,
and women also who have been enslaved by tyrannical men.
This god (or was it Cupid) visited me in a dream (or during the day,
I can't be sure)
and spoke these words, *Ovid, you who write books on the Art of
Love*
and alternately these poems on the Cures for Love
add this maxim to your own list:
HE WHO REMEMBERS HE WAS TORTURED BY LOVE
WILL BE CURED OF LOVE
All men suffer from problems of one sort or another.
He who gets depressed each month because he can't pay his bills,
torments himself over all the debt he's accumulated.
*A son whose father continues to be abusive will ask the gods for
help.*
And if they don't he will spend the rest of his life in therapy.
*The man who marries a woman without a dowry and as a result
lives in poverty,*
will blame her for his lack of success in life.
*Do you have a fine house, a new Porsche, a swimming pool, all on
credit,*

and you can't sleep at night fearing your ability to pay for it all?
Another man is on a ship coming home from Asia and fears the
raging sea
and imagines his ship crashing into the rocks and all his treasures
scattered on the shore.
Another fears for his son who was shipped to Iraq; a mother
worries her daughter will never marry and provide her with a
grandson.
These examples should make it clear that everyone has causes for
anxiety.
Paris, perhaps you wouldn't have loved Helen if you knew how
your brothers suffered before they died in battle.
The child in the dream was still speaking as he vanished
leaving a brief lingering smell of sulphur behind.
Had I dreamed this? Or was it real?
Where these the words of a god or was it just an auditory
hallucination?
What will I do? Palinurus, drugged by the gods, slipped and fell
into the ocean.
I am now alone at the helm directing the ship over uncharted seas.
Now listen, what I'm going to say is very important for a lover in
pain:
SHUN SOLITUDE.
It is very dangerous to be alone.
Why go back to an empty room when you can spend the day at a
café talking with your friends. It's safer to be in a crowd.
Alone, you'll torment yourself. You'll see her face before you
in a vision that seems so real
and ask yourself questions about the relationship like, "What went
wrong?"
or "Was I to blame."
The night is harder for you than the day.
Your friends have gone home, some to their wives,
and for you there is no one to ease your mind.
Still, don't go back to that empty room. Don't shut yourself inside.

Don't turn away from the world and hide in the shadows
even though you've been crying.
Invite your friends to your apt., talk to them about it, they'll
understand.
There is always a Pylades out there to comfort his Orestes. Call on a
best friend.
Think of Phyllis alone in the woods and remember what happened
to her.
Without a doubt, the lack of a friend was the cause of her death.
She ran towards the shore her hair flowing wildly, like a
madwoman,
looking like one of the Bacchantes who celebrate the festival of
Bacchus
every three years in the Aeolian Hills.
She gazed out at the sea like a woman possessed, hoping to see his
ship,
and sometimes she flung herself onto the sand, exhausted,
and wailed like a terrified animal.
She cried out, "Demophoon come back, please, come back, it is my
life you save,"
to the vast silent ocean, tears running down her face.
She could be seen walking along the path that led to the shore,
the tall trees casting shadows all around her.
She walked this path nine times until finally she cried out, "I hate
you."
Her face turned pale as she looked up at the branches,
and placed her long white fingers around her neck.
Then she looked down at the belt around her waist.
She didn't know if this was the right thing to do. She was afraid.
Thracian girl, I regret you were alone at that critical moment.
The trees would have had no reason to weep,
their leaves falling to the ground like teardrops,
if you were still alive.
Now if you're a man rejected by a woman you love
or a woman rejected by a man she loves,

remember the story of Phyllis and know it's never a good idea to be alone.

16

I have almost come to the conclusion of my "cures for love"
but there is one more piece of advice I must give you, as a proper doctor should,
concerning what you may eat and what you should avoid like the plague.
Stay away from anything with a bulbous nature,
whether it's those onions from Italy or Megara or from the shores of Libya.
Even certain mushrooms can excite your desires.
You must also avoid those various concoctions of herbs, plants, spices etc.,
that are generally known as aphrodisiacs. Watch out for all of them,
but especially the one that is popular now in Rome called "Stroke your Rocket."
Better to eat rue, which is good for the eyes,
because what have I been doing in these poems, after all,
except helping you to see clearly what Love's tricks are and to avoid pitfalls.
So keep away from foods that stimulate your desire. Sedatives are what you need.
Many poets have spoken of the curative properties of the sacred vine,
praising Bacchus to no end as they swallow bottle after bottle of the intoxicating liquid.
And so, briefly: Wine is a kind of aphrodisiac and is sure to stimulate the desire for sex,
provided you're not so intoxicated that you can't stand up!
Breezes keep the flame burning; heavy winds put it out.
So don't touch that bottle if you just want a few sips.

If you must, drink until all your troubles vanish or until you fall
asleep.
If you ignore my warning and have a few casual drinks over the
course of a night,
you will do more harm than good and you'll end up right where you
started (in her bed!).
My cures will not have worked.
Now I conclude my *Cures for Love*
and I wish all you young men and pretty girls the best of luck!
It was a long perilous journey, dear reader, but I have safely
reached the shore.
Crown my boat with garlands!
Give thanks to your poet, Ovid, and wish him well
so that he too may have success in love!

GAINED IN TRANSLATION: A PREFACE TO 20 RUSSIAN POETS

Here is a bouquet – an ikebana of sorts – of Russian poetic voices in my not-so-humble translation. Of these twenty, most are prominent poets, several are recently risen ones, and three or four are extremely popular (notably including Dennis Novikov, 1967-2004). Today's Russian poetry is vast, brilliant, obsessive, and highly competitive. It has a distinct, unique character, richly informed by the entire Russian poetic tradition and to a lesser degree by the more recent influence of Western (not least of all American) poetry, available to post-Soviet Russian speakers in the original and in translation. One feature that will leap to the eye is that Russian poetry has not lost (and is unlikely ever to lose) its tremendous formal vigor. Its intimate connections with its own past have never been severed to the same extent as they have been in the West.

Briefly put, Russian poetry not only generates innovative change, but also absorbs and incorporates it, makes use of it. This process remains a source of its vitality. In 1912, the Futurist manifesto titled "A slap in the Face of Public Taste" (signed by David Burliuk, Alexei Kruchenykh, Vladimir Mayakovsky, and Velimir Khlebnikov) demanded: "Throw Pushkin, Dostoevsky, Tolstoy, and so on and so forth, overboard from the Ship of Modernity. He who does not forget his first love will not find his last." It is a sentiment that brings a smile a century later. But the manifesto's demand introduces a significant new idea, that literature is temporal, historical, and therefore also temporary, subject to death, to peeling off. This view opposes the older traditional belief, still held by a good many Russian poets, that poetry's values and highest accomplishments are in some sense timeless. On the new view, there is a first love and there is a last love, and time hurtles, as straight as the arrow flies, from antiquity toward modernity, leaving behind everything that it passes. In the

91

West, such demands for a radical modernity tended in the 20th century to result in a splitting of poetic cultures into opposing, politicized camps. Poetry camps inevitably develop their own dogmatic fetishisms and attempts at formulating alternative canons. Programmatic camp-mongering seems to be enabled by liberal democracies. It is passé today, at least here in US poetry, with its apparent formal anarchy, where what were once militant and unsettling aesthetic-political initiatives are now suitably institutionalized and reconciled under the relativist ethic of redundant diversity, as if in a big literary supermarket heavily stocked with remaindered books. Meanwhile, Russia was for much of the past century a scene of totalitarian political oppression, and under its current regime it has returned to totalitarianism, censorship, political prisoners, political assassinations and all. Russian poetry, with its tradition of resisting and opposing totalitarianism, is united by its humanity, has never "forgotten its first love," and has not splintered into antagonistic camps.

Russian poetry has incorporated its avantgarde on friendly and intimate terms. The genius of Khlebnikov influenced Mayakovsky and (to a lesser but important extent) Osip Mandelshtam, blending indelibly through them into Russian poetry's gene pool. The OBERIU movement of the 1920s-30s (Nikolai Zabolotsky, Daniil Kharms, Alexander Vvedensky, Nikolai Oleinikov, and others) has likewise influenced a great deal of Russian verse. While the avantgarde undoubtedly exists as an identifiable tradition (indeed, traditions, plural) in Russian poetry, the more mainstream tendencies of Russian verse have never played second fiddle to the avantgarde in terms either of formal evolution and innovation or of political robustness. The Russian avantgarde, in turn, has never abandoned the use of traditional poetic forms for its own purposes. Unlike in the US, in post-Stalin Russia there has never been any significant political or personal antagonism between experimental and lyric poets. Nor do Russian poets see differences in aesthetic practice as meaningful obstacles to friendship or to liking each other's work. Several important post-

perestroika poetic groups and movements, such as the Almanac
Poetry Group and the Poetry Club of the latter 1980s and early
1990s, included both traditional and experimental poets, many of
whom remain personal friends to each other to this day.

What has never truly caught on in Russian letters is the
Western idea of the poet as the dry, wry postmodern ironist who
undermines and deconstructs poetry, poking clever fun at it with
an antinostalgic, clinical heart and exposing poetry's presumably
ridiculous nature and alleged complicity in the bourgeois status
quo. This model has proven to be of little interest to Russian poets,
perhaps because their lifestyles, attitudes and social positions
are typically far from bourgeois. Even the most subversive
"conceptualist" hijackers of Russian verse, D. A. Prigov (1940-
2007) and Lev Rubinstein, are at times touched with an authentic
tragic fire.

Free verse has become well acclimatized in the Russian
language over the past three decades. Today, free verse (mostly
known by its French nickname of *vers libre*) has carved out its
own aesthetic space in Russian and no longer feels strange to most
poetry readers. Incidentally, Russia's top student of free verse, Yury
Orlovsky, has been publishing essential research into all aspects
of it. To my mind, the formal situation in Russia today is the
reverse of what we observe on these shores. Here in the US, most
poets use free verse by default, only occasionally dabbling in "trad
forms," while the "formalist" poets constitute a small minority. In
Russia, those poets who chiefly use free verse remain a minority,
although many formal poets write more than an occasional free
verse poem. Moreover, Russian free verse has a distinguishing
quality, frequently lost in underequipped translation, a quality that
is due to its being written by poets with "perfect pitch," as it were,
i.e. poets whose ears are finely attuned to meter and rhyme in all
their exacting, endless possibilities. (Such fine formal versification
skills have now mostly been lost by American poets, who, though
with brilliant exceptions, often sound nondescript, naïve or
downright "mauvist" when they sporadically attempt to show off

their command of traditional verse.) Technically speaking, this kind of fine-tuned free verse shares with formal poetry the sense of a fixed time (as in music). Its lines tend to be variously metrical or rhythmically patterned, rather than oblivious of poetic meter. In this regard, Russian free verse is akin in its sound, not to the more amorphous varieties of contemporary American free verse, but to the free verse composed by such original pioneers as Eliot, Crane, Lowell, cummings and others, who were also outstanding masters of regular verse, blessed with a perfect metrical sense).

Even given the constraints of space, the present selection conveys some idea of Russian poetry's geography. Several of the twenty are Moscow poets, while the others live in the Russian provinces (including Tatarstan and the Caucasus) and in the diaspora (Ukraine, Israel, and the US). A great deal of important Russian poetry is written outside the borders of today's Russia. Unfortunately, Russian culture today, both at official and unofficial levels, is characterized by a xenophobic, anti-Western, and anti-émigré prejudice. Emigration is especially demonized and seen as a form of treason by many patriotic, politically loyal Russians. (So far as I can tell, this attitude is uniquely Russian. By contrast, China loves its émigrés and fosters good relations with them.) That said, this prejudice is less felt in poetry, or at least among the poets that matter.

In this century, the global reach of the Internet and of social media, along with the openness of Russia's more cosmopolitan literary presses and prizes to the work of Russophone poets abroad, Russian poetry has for the first time ever been able to consolidate itself into a coherent, wired global whole that stays abreast of itself in real time. This is a major new development. Back in the pre-perestroika days of "advanced socialism" (a.k.a. "the period of stagnation"), we poets who lived in the USSR at the time would receive as an epiphany every new poem by Joseph Brodsky, smuggled in across the Iron Curtain. "Congratulations, we have a new Brodsky poem!" we would say to each other. Similarly, it was practically impossible for émigré poets closely to follow poetic developments in Russia. But today, when any Russophone online lit rag uploads a new issue, folks in St. Petersburg or and Novosibirsk, in Tel Aviv and New York can read it right away. State borders no longer apply in poetry.

Or do they? Will this healthy freedom of communication, this international Russophone poetic milieu, endure? A witch hunt for "agents of Western influence" has been going on in Russia since 2012. Most recently, on May 1 of this year 2019, Vladimir Putin signed into law the bill "on Sovereign RuNet," giving the Russian authorities the legal power to isolate the Russian cyberspace from the rest of the world, on the Chinese model. The new law officially entered into force on November 1, 2019. The Kremlin is eager to isolate Russia from the West both politically and culturally and to stem the tide of Western Russophone influence, felt strongest via literature, journalism, and social media. If such a digital isolationism is implemented, Russian poetry may again find itself artificially divided. But when have such concerns ever stopped tyrants from doing what they do?

Philip Nikolayev
Cambridge, MA

OLGA CHUGAI (1944-2015)

That which your hands
Have touched
Has since perished.
Slowly the fire of life
Turns all that lives to black dust.
However, all that your heart
Has touched
And cherished
Has survived. Only love
Lives longer than us.

Philip Nikolayev

The Shed

It isn't true! Even on your knees,
Eyes closed, repeating
A prayer or a simple request
Aimed at heaven, know that you will get
Nothing, zero,
And will not see or grasp
Anything at all.
Some thirty years ago,
A child was weeping in the darkness of a shed,
Kneeling on some freshly sawn
Sweet smelling birch planks,
A green sunray
Reaching through a chink in the wall
Toward the tear-streaked face
Framed in flaxen curls. There was no fear
As the words of the child's prayer –
That solitary request – hung in the air
Without vanishing as large hawk moths
Orbited the lamppost right next to the shed.

Philip Nikolayev

DENNIS NOVIKOV (1967-2004)

The warrior wishes to relax; the raven wants to eat
and misinterprets sleep as death, as something that it's not.
Mislead by his declining sight, confused by mere repose!
Everyone's going blind. That's right. Ravens? Yes, even those.
And so it goes on from the start for the full course of time:
when one's asleep, another must foresee a corpse in him,
as if the black wing raven were the wolf within the man,
while you who spend the night with him serve as a restaurant.
But I've been asked to pass the word: the warrior must sleep
And, waking, must keep sliding back into the dreamy deep.

you are dealing today with a different man
who no longer supposes himself
oscar wilde home from gaol with a lifeless old cane
and a sinister rot on his lip
why are fate's rented rooms always furnished like crap
uninviting and sad to the max
while the artist forever gets played for a sap
by rank wannabes ignorant brats

ALEXEI TSVETKOV

schoenberg in brentwood

so strike the umlaut from the family name
as handel did on finding fame abroad
amid the dressy palms and bougainvillea
the pilgrim's virgil is a trusty ford
in one of the vague snapshots of the era
the garden hose is craning its giraffe
neck avidly toward tropical flora
across the dull grain of the photograph
was it in purgatorio that dante
incited us to chant cantos andante

a weirder neighbor not half a mile from here
is hard to find in fable or in truth
he who was once the darling of his era
but later booed and catcalled by the youth
observe the soul up to its gills in fatness
and clinging fondly to its glorious past
on a seashore where the sky is a necklace
of the twelve twinkling zodiacal notes
who said that life was scary and no fun
it's barely one year old and nearly gone

the longcase clock chimes heavily thirteen in
a paradise the heavens echo back
with the cia and the old gold guarding lion
the ford dies in the morn of heart attack
unfortunate whose rusty wheels are more so
of baggage and of passengers bereft
while by the gateway a witness from warsaw
gives testimony that they have all left

Philip Nikolayev

enter the garden hum the haunting bars
and realize you've forgotten these stars

there's no leader just tendinous murmur
the twelve brave tones are left to die alone
in sinai's heat forget the fuck your schoenberg
look in the mirror in the passport man
off with the head if you can't shrink the syndrome
with lore of oxbridge or of the sorbonne
but there's a homeland where work promises freedom
and there is moses but no way back home
the horns well marked by michelangelo
form an umlaut upon your head's o

Elegy for the Teddy Bear

sweet hearsay tell me google let me know
where does the plush teddy bear go
when his upholstered back has worn threadbare
all white with age and it is shining plain
that life was a mistake ie in vain
or maybe even not at all poor bear
the beads have fallen from the sightless eyes
someone explain why he is leaving us

under the couch in that dim senior home
he waited mute for them to come for him
and now we see him milling by the entrance
dragging a bit behind his busted foot
soon enough the eternity'll commence
of the great butcher of all plush and soft
cheeks frozen into laughter or in tears
heaven for dolls and inferno for bears

i'll sit down in the bedroom where he dwelt
and briefly into farewell tears will melt
this empty drawer was once his apartment
he won't come back vestige of former joys
couldn't the master of all the world's toys
just patch us up and mend the harm a bit
no one can now collect those torn off paws
or find those eyes groping about the floors

VLADIMIR GANDELSMAN

The Crux of the Matter

The brief moment of falling asleep is
uniquely lovely and light-winged:
first you're awake, then suddenly all this
Laterna Magika is finished, extinguished.

Disrupting the flow of narration
of states of affairs and of things,
we must dwell on our separation
in detailed, mind-numbing imaginings.

So that we may face it without cursing,
no, without any regret at all,
but instead with gratitude, embracing
it. The rest is inessential.

On the Horizon

While the black umbrellas marched on
and autumn sobbed and drizzled,
I suddenly saw my mom on the horizon
of memory, and was dazzled.

I clearly saw the room, the white light –
she had been three years bedridden –
while the black umbrellas marched
in the future, and I stood grief-stricken.

At times she had trouble using her hand
or speaking, to her frustration.
Who is praiseworthy? Only a saint
who does not curse the human condition.

She would peer out the window, to descry,
seemingly, my future life without her
and to graft the sorrows of her own eyes
upon threads of a detailed autumn shower.

so they might return, so they might return,
while autumn churned its tearful song
and the black umbrellas marched on and on,
dazzling me on the horizon.

MIKHAIL AYZENBERG

The sleepwalker forgotten in the night's
vastness, alone in front of the tall gates,
is desperate to pick the key that matches,
harassed by shades with unfamiliar features
that are like kin he fails to recognize.

The past, however dreamt, is bent on voyage,
new destinations seem to be its wish.
A pain that is too large to fit a visage
whirs toward us like a bird from a bush.

Finding the needle, I wonder if it was
lurking not my heart, but in a haystack.

So shed some light on this with one of those
camp flashlights with enduring batteries,
reliable in the midst of a night train wreck.

Philip Nikolayev

Tonight displays not soft-lit bedroom shatters
but tiny, evilly conspiring glares
until such time as it collapses, scatters
into sharp smithereens of shattered air.

We're not asleep. We are busy. We don't
exist, standing immobile under water
deep on a riverbed, hearing forever
untimely telephones calling us to account.

LEV RUBINSTEIN

Winter Vacation

One day we were hanging out together
And the next day Yuri Stepanov
Didn't show up at school
What's the matter what's up with that?

On the way home I ran
Into Nina Nikolaevna
With a shopping bag Yuri's mom
He is ill she said has a high fever

The next day was a short day
We had only two classes
The others had been cancelled
As winter break was starting

In the first class we read from a book
About the war hero Leonid Golikov
And during the second our grade sheets
Were handed out and off we went home

We decided to pay our ill comrade
A visit the three of us were
Smirnov and I and for some reason Tanya
Chvileva a straight-A student

On the way we bought
A hematogen bar at the pharmacy
For the patient we each took a tiny bite
But left the rest for him

Philip Nikolayev

Wiping our feet on arrival we removed
The galoshes and found Yuri in his bed
Cheery and ruddy with fever we handed
Him his grades they were all Cs

And Nina Nikolaevna goes in a merry voice
And did I not tell him to wear his long johns
He never listens he never puts them on
And there you go you can see the result

Smirnov and I exchanged a look
While Tanya the straight-A girl
Turned crimson and Yuri glared
At his mom as in how could you mom

How can you mention long johns
In front of girls you can't
You just can't you can't
You cannot do this mom

When we left it dawned on us that
The treat meant for our ill comrade
Was still with us and we divided it fairly
And ate it and the winter vacation started

VIKTOR KOVAL

Bucolic

A battle of grackles
with cussing grackle calls
concerning each other or
the tractor operator
with Tchaikovsky's first concerto
on the transistor radio,
with Richter at the piano
and von Karajan – oh –
conducting
the whole darn thing.
No one seems thrilled.
OK, that's it, it's over.
The players are afield!
The soccer match begins.

VITALY PUHANOV

Existential

The vodka finished, we have cashed in
The empties and have had enough,
Ready for our heads to be bashed in.
What else can you expect from life?

Your bed will be a wooden plank.
No lunch! Lunches don't grow on trees
And "luck" forever rhymes with "fuck,"
Though the philologist disagrees.

Mushroom Season

One day you'll go alone into the woods,
Where we have gone a thousand times together,
Where honey mushrooms still protrude their goods
On the same spot the same day of the year.
You'll slice them off the tree stump with my knife or
Reach for a cigarette (but you can't find your lighter),
Look helplessly about the forest floor,
Blaming me for the fact that I'm no more.
Leaving the basket where you couldn't find me,
You will head home, not hearing me behind you.

NINA GABRIELYAN

The Early Reaper

> *"...And I awoke, and I arose..."*
> *Konstantin Erznkatsi (c. 1250 – c. 1314)*

Rise, go into the blue fields at predawn
With new daylight's first stalks in the distance
Where a solitary early reaper
Is at work in the mists of existence

As she walks over planets and stars
On the edge between darkness and light
In the space between sky and blue earth
To the radiance where they almost meet.

Follow then between lightness and dark
In her footsteps unhurriedly:
It's the path on which you must embark
Out of time to eternity.

The Builder

I'm in no rush, I know that it will come.
I'm not building a temple but a stairway.
I'm in no hurry, I will wait my turn
To roll downstairs and bruise my knees one day,
To smash with my own weight my fragile frame,
To reconstruct myself, bone by crushed bone.
What will come true someday, for now is false.
Though it is light, night isn't far away.
I'm building, not a temple, but a stairway:
There is no ceiling and there are no walls.

Philip Nikolayev

SERGEI PREOPBRAZHENSKY (1955-2017)

Avantgarde

Big letters in posters glow merry and red.
The yardman has typhus, already half dead.
The courtyard's in snow, the Commander-in-Chief's
Rolls-Royce is advancing along the grill fence.

The square prewar model aggressively roaring,
An order is barked in the barracks to fall in.
His speech will be brief, and his obvious rubric
Is going to be: "We Must Save the Republic!"

One poster portrays -- with invention and force --
A snaggle-toothed Denikin on a white horse:
A hefty Red Armyman firmly says "Nyet!"
And threatens him good with his red bayonet.

"Yes, artists, like soldiers, are tools of the masses!
Now isn't the season for rose-colored glasses,
When history's ready to turn a new leaf!"
Thought in the Rolls-Royce the Commander-in-Chief.

A tool of the masses, bohemian bloke
and VKhUTEMAS student, inhales hand-rolled smoke
And deftly exhales revolutionist charm,
A fresh toothy poster rolled under his arm.

The slogan is cheery, its lettering red.
The yardman is dying. His daughter, in dread,
Has lit a new candle, is praying and crying
And crossing herself, or at any rate trying.

Now he who worked daily to build you a haven
In this murky basement as if in bright heaven
Lies cradling an icon in his lifeless breast.
You say, Revolution? He isn't impressed.

The young avantgardist's heroic
New posters will save the Rebublic,
And Pavel Filonov's canvasses
Reveal the bared teeth of the masses.

Surveillance Face

The man of stainless alloy atop the towering column
Tilts his surveillance face into the street below and stares.
He has been soaring there for an long, long time,
Thickly sprinkled with the immobile pollen of stars.

I've passed numerous times directly beneath his flight,
Hundreds of prehensile seconds under the titan wingspan
Ticking away in the heartrending silence of night,
All counted by pipistrelle bats with dogged persistence.

How adamant is your impressive armored brow ridge,
O you who have learned by rote the stasis of freefall
And whose well-lit hand is equipped to detect and gauge
The metal pulse of my blood, decomposably moral.

As metallic love's electrical rumbling escalates,
Your airtight flight lifts off to breathless heights,
Heading toward the axial section of wolfish lanes
Where my desired woman sleepily resides

And where I too, like a visitant pilot from outer space,
Will be able to lower into her my surveillance face,
So that in her sleep she may soar above the abyss,
Watching the Milky Way splitting to fragments, bits.

OLGA BRAGINA

all right not dead but could be living more intensely
the high A key always gets stuck in the song about Lorelei
this language is hardly for love for it only spares the umlaut
first roses burst into bloom in a window trimmed with frost
couplet three says that there's no one else here but us word eaters
who taste the fruit of forbidden flesh and hang on tighter than burs
I'm clueless what's happened to me it's a heresy not worth thinking
like a hangman's man hanged head down still clinging to meaning
but consequently since I am not yet dead I could finish reading
Heine
under an arterially cracked plexiglas but sadly hardly anyone
recalls how the comb burned the palm or broke on rocks its teeth
the translator mayn't be half bad but these shallows are too deep
and if I definitely ain't dead just a tad purple in the jaw the kinder-
garten naps no one throws pillows into the abyss to grasp what's in
there
no one is stepping into a brook no one's drawing hills in a drawing
book
which brims with no prophecy and will never come true for us to
see
so and now let's listen to the Four Seasons shall we

prefabricated concrete eyesores shall remain
the landmarks of your haunted windowpane,
along with passersby in black from the chinese
commodity markets. i've read the to-do list, with ease
forgetting it. marching in a column, they'll walk
past the construction warehouse and back
to where i'd truly have loved to find some wet
matches in the melting snow and tried, but failed,
striving for so many years to quit smoking.
as the roman orator said... never mind, it's boring.
folks walk out the brightly lit supermarket,
plastic bags filled with cabbage heads. let
more water dissolved in port spill on snow. ah yes,
must remember to buy matches and roller bandages.

IYA KIVA

gender identity issues

my friend says i have gender identity issues
i want to feel androgynous
i need to buy new sneakers
gotta go to Kiev's Voskresenka area to General Vatutin Street
i don't want to be part of a family of a community or of social
                    stratification
i just want to have the opportunity to come out for a run
which is why i try on a manicure and feminine models of behavior
while thinking of how the color black or white can be pink
and experience gender as danger the danger of collapsing through
it
but even at the opposite end of the city i am unable to find the right
size
and i fail to discover myself in the body of a man or woman
i fail to discover my own body in a man or woman
i fail to discover a man in the body of a woman
i fail to discover a man in the body of a man
i fail to discover a woman in the body of a man
and don't know where else to go looking for those dratted sneakers
thinking about it in the pauses between reading and work
i don't know what to do if I end up having to go outside
i don't know what to do with this heap of clothes for an alien body
i don't know i to feel i wanna i no understand

ANDREI TOROPOV

We read our Salinger when we were eighteen,
Dostoevsky, Kafka, Camus, and others,
We know how to bend, to grovel, to demean
Ourselves, while asking "Why?" with the eyes.

Why? Just because love is always stronger,
Just because it will surely come no matter
What, though it hurts the more the longer
It takes, with its sign: "Extreme Danger! Enter!"

It's the last idea we can save in words
And sleep with ever after, with some luck;
Apart from that, we are deaf, blind, and idiot birds,
Woodcocks lekking. Hey, come join the lek!

Philip Nikolayev

We'll never age to be too old,
Like Thyl or Nele, or like poems;
We'll merely turn rich, fat, and bald,
Hoarders of too much junk in homes.
The years will work their magic on us,
Yet they are powerless to reverse
Or tame the liberties of youth,
The stupid treasure troves of verse.

EVGENY MOROZOV

The Kid

Skinny, adolescent, he'd enter unobtrusively,
softly say hello, look people in the face
inquiring "How's life?" and sit in a corner,
quietly present, rustling a magazine.
Having trouble pronouncing his r's and l's,
he would ask plainly about things and God,
looking at you the way children look,
poignant and pure and clueless.
The politeness of a southern sea lay dozing
in his eyes of living mother of pearl
while the sluggishness of graystone was
starting to awaken within his tranquility.
One is expected to be nimbler at seventeen,
but he was underweight and a weakling:
a rash of zits, a crewcut, angular shoulders,
a sweater the color of ash. They said of him
that he had "a retardation," but gave him
no offensive nicknames. He went to
a special needs school, but was kind
and selfless, unlike his aggressive classmates.
Him being the oldest of three sons,
the other two had the same crewcuts,
wore gray and had trouble pronouncing
the same letters. Except that the youngest
was slightly different, darker-skinned
and seemingly scared, and the middle one
seemed the liveliest of the lot
and more interested in talking to folks.
They seldom showed up together, mostly
two or one at a time. They'd say hi

and keep silent and not smile,
hanging close to each other.
One day a man paid them a visit,
redfaced and in a green jumper.
Offering a broad and powerful hand, he
introduced himself softly: "I'm your father."

The Toy Horse

He was a kid much like other kids, ruddy-cheeked,
jug-eared, cobalt-eyed, 8-year-old or so,
perhaps a bit older, attending school, already
starting to ask his first awkward questions.

His protective mother fed him and bought him
clothes as well as many fascinating toys,
including a large plastic horse on wheels
that you could mount and ride a short distance.
And the child fell in love with the horse
and called it his "pony," petted it, cherished it,
fed it plastic oranges and even combed
its hard surface with a wooden comb.
But when he lost the keys to the apartment,
his mother got upset and scolded him loudly,
chased him around the room with a belt,
and ended up throwing away the toy horse.
It's a good thing that his dad kept his cool,
changed the lock in the door, gave him a candy,
and then undressed and went to sleep
on the sofa, smelling like hospital injections.

But even dad wasn't always in a good mood.
The kid realized that after accidentally
breaking an expensive cassette player,
for which he received a painful flick on the nose.
But it's a good thing that he was attending school,
where he could amuse himself with his friends,
who were not always bullying him and didn't
take his pocket money away from him every day.
The boy grew quite tall as the years went by,
took a job, got himself a dog, a girlfriend,
a new apartment and a nice speedy car.

His friends were often inviting him to parties,
for old times' sake, to remember school, they said,
but he always refused with the words:
"No, you used to take away my pocket money!"
His dad, now gray-haired and working from home,
would invite him to come visit, to catch up.
And he did, but no more than twice a year,
grumbling: "You flicked me on the nose!"
And folks always said nice things about his
late mother, reminiscing about the past
whenever they ran into him in the street.
He expressed his agreement with everything,
while thinking: "She murdered my pony..."

ALEXEI ALEXANDROV

The hotel comes with breakfast included,
As to lunch, it is well past my budget,
So the mouth feels a Sartrean brooding,
Premonitions of terror and bloodshed.

Why has someone unplugged from the wall
The worn cord of the clothes-pressing iron?
Furs emerge out of long estivation
In sleep-stupid boutiques in the fall.

Here, no parlormaid, only the plumber
And the public committee – oh bummer –
Climb the stairwell to rap on your door.
The beasts snore, birchwood smoke everywhere.

As your permanent partner-at-arms
Has half-woven your funeral wreath,
The long bathhouse and laundry day burns
To a telephoned grief, out of breath.

It's the dad of two smartass teen daughters
Checking in to confirm, verify
The stamped seal, where the sign says, "Disturb Us!"
But the boys are too scared to scoot by.

It is possible, inserting your hand into a sack,
to pull out nothing but a toolkit, to drink
a quantity of kvass to cope with hunger.

Crop failures, the bird that totally looks
like a burned shrub, and the kind words
of technical support, all flake in tufts.

Because the sun, the river and the wind
are fear, grief, and ultimate despair of
explaining anything to the focus group.

These are not mere difficulties
of translation; these are arrows
and pictograms, basic colors and sounds.

Philip Nikolayev

YANISLAV WOLFSON

The Last Boat Ride

Were my parents still numbered among the living,
I would take them for a boat ride on a river,
A calm and average one and not too wide,
Under a triangular sailcloth sail.

The stream would go on meandering and weakening
Between its two vodka-guzzling banks, but deliver
A reward, extending our laughable lifespans by an unspecified
Duration, involuntarily yet without fail.

Taking the dwindling of wind as a form of betrayal,
The bruise of sunset still swelling in the celestial puddle,
I would turn my boat's best flank to the land in farewell,
Having untied every knot, overcome every last muddle.

Shackled by silence and windlessness, we would all just sit there,
Underachieving students in a long geometry class,
Memorizing every inch of the creeping shadow, choosing not to stare
Back at the amassed burdens and laments of the past.

We would talk of strange places, of mysterious voyages,
Mention the map's farthest corners and the scale of bigness,
And I, guilty of many things, would jump on this chance to apologize,
And yes, they would majestically grant me their forgiveness.

I would so love to while away the remaining minutes,
So I imagine, under a stirless sail that glides unbidden,
In a simple boat that's steered by my son by instinct,
As if we had no use for words either spoken or written.

And now that the shrunken swirl of sunset has thoroughly bled
Into the heavy waters and even the banks fade from sight,
My pencil-sharpening fear cedes the seat reserved for the disabled
Peaceably to the eternal night.

GALI-DANA SINGER

The Ballad of Invisible Ink

– But you must remain silent about everything that you see here, –
I declared one dark rusty night
and repeated one fine lunar day.
A shabby evening turned into the gray
windy willow of a morning.

– But you must remain silent about everything that you see here, –
I kept reiterating with ellipsis dots.
Death led, like the dotted line
of a pulse, away and out of sight,
the whole firmament undulating.

– But you must remain silent about everything that you see here, –
as I stood, eyes shut,
in the heart of a white
flame, a gloomy chiming
rang out loud behind me:

– But you must remain silent about everything that you see here, –
with the sky as my bedsheet,
with the dusk as my blanket,
my whole bed felt
chilling and boring.

– But you must remain silent about everything that you see here, –
striking a flinty spark
of insincerity,
I slandered my own art,
burning the dictionary.

– But you must remain silent about everything that you see here, –

enduring the allure just fine,
but in no rush to pay the fine,
I now pour colorless ink
upon the paper's silk.

ALEXANDER PAVLOV

storage room

estival wenches are wearing out of season things
hibernal ones fresh snow autumnal ones lips of mercury
while vernal witches kill you dead with scorpion stings
locking you into a single-decker monogamy
the merry-go-round falls asleep its bright kitschy gloss
arrested in its tracks but a street song blasts the sky
god escapes from champagne with a pop like gas
coffins of love on the curb thwart the progress of skis
the swollen sore throat is fitting for january's
antique drunken gigue under the lost lamppost
on which the wandering jew peruses heart attack x-rays
who these days wears them in pairs more often than most

silence serum

at eventide a sudden bat scratches past the light
a watermelon odor spreads like our savior
the altar soon to fall silent as flickering bright
majolicas spring from lit hay a familiar behavior
while you stand drenched in dew as beat as a threshold
breaking the cuckoo's out in the woods brittle count
a falling star scatters in the eye its rippling gold
itself a ripe ashberry red so the eye is stunned
and a sortie of swifts of the air over and above a
crumpled dream in twilight they overfly
a spot where love has run out but the lover
still hears the bells that go deaf being drunk on sky

YULY GUGOLEV

Rage

Again, the milieu is enraged,
but the food's taste's unchanged,
and water's keen to spew its wrath
without leaving the mouth.

Isn't there something we could do
in spite of such sad trends,
by joining ranks without ado
with our like-minded friends?

It can be anything at all
our friends and we could do,
join ranks, lock arms and walk awol,
hobo abreast of hobo.

The cage door shuts no matter what,
there's no more "no," nor "yes."
Truthless, the world ends in the twat
of its big universe.

So, what's the moral? Must we pass,
submissive biomass,
like herds regurgitating grass,
silent into the past

as powerlines stretch in long strands
toward a nowhere night
and overhead a band of clouds
floats perilously bright?

Translator's note: Russia has recently banned cuss-words from print and public media.

POLINA BARSKOVA

Summer Camp Chant

A cold June in a "Young Pioneer" summer camp:
At night the rains cause whole dorms of kids
To wet their beds and in the morning the comp-
Romized bedsheets (did
Someone say Rothko?) are hung –
By way of a shaming and disciplining gesture –
Behind the Lenin-as-child statue
By the tall bush burning with lilacs that is its own king.

Every cluster of lilac blossoms still dangles
Over my face at a hopeless angle,
Like that dream involving the handsome camp counselor
Who ignored me the entire summer,
Or like that desperate, failed
Attempt at letter to my parents, left unmailed,
Permanently lost among the ghosts
Of the perfectly completed past.

Whenever I yearn to tell my American-born
daughter about my Russian past, it all
Turns out to be ineffable, untranslatable: I can't
Express the golden-haired Ulyanov/Lenin kid
And have no equivalent for our quaint
Terms for "canteen" and "camp chant."
Time, as if sifted though irony's sieve, is received
By the addressee
As a distant cold light, approximate and fuzzy.

Yes, exactly: those faded Victorian photos
Of immaterial spirits and disembodied ghosts
Are either all fake or, on the contrary, a most sincere

Philip Nikolayev

Plea, verging on a stark prophetic oracle –
An unmailed letter: "Please take me the hell away from here!" –
Where the ghost cringes in the daguerreotype,
Like a lilac bunch pregnant with the sky,
Neither trusting in nor denying any miracles.

Philip Nikolayev

OK

The poet works with the tongue.

The translator works with the uvula.

31 years ago there was a moderately sized cat of my acquaintance.

The degree of our acquaintanceship needn't be exaggerated,
But he would drop by once in a while to find out exactly how much
I had missed him.
On one such visit he jumped in from the garden veranda, only to
find me sleeping.
What followed amazed me. I began to realize, through sleep, that
someone
Was licking my sweaty enormous July face
Methodically all over, centimeter by centimeter.

The artistry of the work was truly worthy of Filonov's brush,
An exercise in "madeness."
Highly ticklish, incredibly laughter-inducing.

The translator is a wee tomcat with part of a fern frond behind the
ear,
Stripping the words of their alien semantic layers,
Shipping them from one dimension's mansion
To another's word by word,
Word shadow by word shadow,
Across a wide web of words.

A slow, salty, ticklish feat of heroism.
I open my eyes, the cat watching me: so close,
So tired, so pleased with his own work as he jumps
Back through the window,
Disappearing.

POEMS

David Blair

THE ARMIES OF BEING HERE TO ETERNITY

Maybe a college graduate or a student,
chunky clubby on hands and knees
squirts tasty bleach on the pedestals
of her exercise job purgatory
as if a boxer aimed his spit
at the gym floor
where Montgomery Clift
as Pvt. Robert E. Lee Prewitt
with spacy demented eyes
kept plucking dandelion violets
from the floors of physical health
where people bring their sad bodies,
and cell phones, and the half-employed
get their euphoria and their yas yas out.

David Blair

POETRY OF FRIENDSHIP

Tom Yuill and I were dressed
in our blue blazer camouflage,
but I was wearing grey pants
and he was wearing a pink dress shirt
in honor of preppie acid heads
from the swim team in Dallas.
We were running late for work
so got a cab over by the city hall,
one of those red ones with a top hat
and cane on the side door,
some town that jacks you on fares,
Brookline cab, not a green Shamrock.
The driver liked Pushkin and all talk
and probably liked Boris Godunov
and since we were talking about Schwab,
our 401's, our portfolios, the bread,
he figured we were stone Republicans.
"No, man," Tom said. "We're professors.
We're trained critical thinkers.
We can't do that shit."
This got the driver c r a z y.
"What do you mean?
What do you mean?
What do you mean?"
His pupils turned blood yellow.
His tongue flickered in the air.
"You mean you are brain-washed!"
"No, man, we know how to think
and read between the lines of texts.
Look, we know where information
comes from and what it looks like. Period."
Then the driver popped his head off

with his two hands and a jet of steam
shot out of his neck. It was just awful
when he started snapping at the steam
and chomping at his shoulders.
"What do you know? I lived
under Communism. Fools.
You are professor fools."
We were at a red light,
Nothing left but a pair of legs
on the front seat and a head
coughing in the leaves, coffee cup lids
and receipts, some of those beads
on the loose up there with a radio,
the jaws stuck on a steering wheel lock
which was like a big nasty tuning fork.
Luckily, we were near the hospitals,
so we could get another cab,
or it was close enough to walk.
There was nothing left to tip,
but I swiped my card,
punched in plenty
to apologize for brains,
stupid ones, crazy ones,
mean ones, smart ones,
all except the kind parts.

SHORT TIME

for James Kealey

1.

Forget the piety and your pious responses
because if you write an elegy long enough,
it becomes another way to say hello, somehow,
until you collapse on the couch in your clothes.

2.

The Chinese restaurant on the corner was called Nice Food.
For years it was like this. We never fought once.

We just stood there talking. And then one of us would fall over.
That was what life was like.

And she was all going around the
room, waving her hands, maybe
conducting stuff. To me, she was like
some Glinda the Good Witch.

And then if one of us fell over, the other was not even looking away,
just watching. Bright. Sometimes, you can catch somebody
tumbling,

and sometimes you just don't. The both of us smelled like her
wings
there, pleasant with its pure water with its pee, hard work, and

6.

The early Romantics did not have such nice shoes. They were like flats, and if some wore boots, they were sort of pigeon deals. They would go walking out in the winter nights of torch-lit university towns, especially if the snow was blue, and then look at those cobble stones going down, or that hard icy curb between the curb and the cobblestones. These shoes have got to get with it, the future. This walking here will just about kill me if I don't really concentrate where I put my feet, o shit.

BIG FAMILY POEM

for my sisters
& brother

1. Wanted Poster

In all the blab
and pork chop
and love
and hate,
we need solitude
and silence, too.

2. Waiting for the Women's March

Bad dynamic. He thinks, young pelican, I feed you fish,
and you go out in the night with that big red hair.

He stands with his glass of wine in the dining room
trying to get as much of his ass as possible

over the heat register in the corner.

Midnight, every night, the guy in his hoodie
throws a spitty tennis ball to his German shepherd.

Bad translation. They kept reading it, "like watching
Kung Fu again," academic somehow, hardly flowing.

He thought he might go
to a conservative political rally

146

and wave a skewer
of uncooked SPAM above his head,

what else could go wrong?

For five days, they wore the same
brown corduroy pants.

Ridges were flattening out,
with supplicant creases

in a few odd places.

Mr. Urbano knocked at the tenant's door
on the ground floor. "Jiggle the handle."

Fig tree wrapped out back,
cut out in the pavement

before the fence.

Even though he was safe in 1978,
the late first baseman touched

the runner's knee with his glove,
laughing together, both of them,

in May, afternoon game.

The entire kitchen and sushi bar staff
napped in the dining room for an hour

between lunch and dinner hours.

Still in kitchen whites, she stood
on the giant river blocks casting

for big river carp
while a garbage barge pushed

in one direction and a coal train
rolled at her back.

Domingo sang while tipping
all manner of shells into an illegal hole

in the floor to float away with the tide,
the same tide that shook

the chandeliers' reflections.

The "dumpster guys" were very polite
about making the waiter, cook,

and dishwasher stay open
until three a.m., left a century note.

She goes on up the hill to see her
girlfriend, pounding it on up that hill

in her big winter coat
with fur all up around the hood,

hero of Telemark, badass tonight.

The dancer in a leather jacket
had gotten herself a crew cut that day,

and Victor was ready to recite poems

from *Twenty Love Poems and a Song of Despair.*

To him, the humid morning smells healthy
at the zoo, maybe straw,

maybe mung bean noodles while they soak.

The sidewalk, all that wide expanse
along the black iron bars

of the Little Sisters of the Poor,
then bump bump bump, plenty

of ice on the sidewalk after that, then whomp.

Wearing socks, she toed the cold floor
register grate. That was how it was going

to be for the whole country.

After the show, he says he also raps
and almost jumped up there himself,

wearing construction boots from work
and a vest with a lot of practical pockets.

Midnight, waters running, the guy
in his hoodie throws a spitty tennis ball

to his German shepherd,
next to big piles of ploughed snow.

It is a warm night in winter.
The young people under thirty

are all acting frisky as can be.

They found each other;
by winter's end, we all can turn

to stuffed dolls made of yarn.

Some lean rich people
have short-cropped grey hair

and play squash and run on treadmills
in finished or archaic basements,

by stony foundations, in damp earth.

"Good Lord, I've got the willies," Rimbaud thinks,
fingering a phantom crawl in his head. Lice.

The barbarians knew that the use
of jargon was an expression of shame

but used jargon by the curb, in the woods.

Being in love and being loved, she reached
for her love and thought, "Let me hold that one."

She lost a whole band of ideas, for a moment or more;
they were righteous, too, the first steps in a new land.

3. Endurance of the Absurd

One time two sisters,
nuns actually

in an awful tennis joke
about God and cursing
not based on me
and my baby brother
like Shoney's Big Boy
were road-tripping
and smoking cigarettes,
and the one not driving
kept burping up Diet Coke,
and the brother driving
me got really freaked out
and grouchy, and said,
"Hey there, fuck, sewer breath,
with the decomposition
of household waste
and cleaning supplies
wrapped around the corner
by the Cambridge line
by the monument place
selling headstones, angels,
if I did not find
you remotely sympathetic
I would not locate
the salt of the sea
and breakdown
of aquatic plants
and all manner
of sea life on the waft
of the cargo tankers
into the harbor, nor
the silver grain silos
and panoramas
of livestock left to roam
north of the Red River
along past the mountains

time present/ time past
of turnpikes into corn,
jet fuel in the accordion
to the US Air flight
in the rain to the cloud
belt, the cloud belt
in its sulfurous steel mill
early morning drizzle
reaching the houses
on the hilltops by
desert, prairie, stone
by the river, coffee
and bacon, the locust
trees, the cherry
tomato plant with two
cherry tomatoes,
the first two of the year,
and that old lady, our
great aunt, gone down
to the bushes to find
her morning newspaper
with this sort of stuff."

"Damn.
Open the window,"
said Sister Mary Elephant.

4. What I Believe at Walden Pond

> *"in my heart Walt Whitman's mind"*
> —Gerard Manley Hopkins

A girl micro-pens hand-colored cartoon razor panels into her diary,
fine-hands dialogue bubbles and her prose narration while some guys

blast Donald Vincent's new album, his flow from a boom box
far away enough to sound only nearby coastal undulations.

The highways turn the color of nicotine stains, the lateral roads
and the overpass streets, rustier by bridges festooned with flags

all over again, summer, roads too narrow for trucks, come to the pond,
even some long-fingered bossa nova guitar chords, a friendship picnic,

up around the lifeguard-free bend, two old guys in ball caps, such old shits,
with outboard tilted up, and boat high in water, lines out, golf shirts, can

feel my own shorts crawling, about the same age, about, as a Chinese couple
emerged from spontaneous dip in water, the lady soaked

and laughing in a dress, maybe come from a Baptist church, feeling
renewed, amused, screw rules, go this way, his slacks knotted to shorts.

All smart people come here. I believe a lady who ladles out bean soup
from her zinc pot here, kinder, thriftier, work-smart, family-love people

with enemies. I see a guy read *What Maisie Knew*. I see a lady with moles
read an academic journal with small print, graphs and two columns per page.

I see a couple perform retina scan and thigh exchange in supple leopard-print
trunks though I can't tell whose ass went with whose arms, pure circus.

I see some rashes and dry skin and peppermint pattern belly meat all-gender
thigh because we have to sit in so many clammy places, like Somerville busses.

It is a good place for the nerdy to swing far out here, the law students speaking
with their transitions and paragraphs, and the goof who interrupts the flow

of mutual discourse to say, "wow wow wow," as his partner steps from her dress
towards the water, but hey, man, you get too shady in my poem, come on.

We all think about bacteria, microscopic life, the large and the small,
as the maple pollen swirls its golden, starry shapes on the waters.

And the pond will be closed next week on account of algae from piss.
I believe everybody here, wicked pissers, the babies especially.

SIMONE DUVALIER

Do your own thing, as the stars do not
necessarily tell you: here is where you
will be after the rocky place you come
from: daughter of mulatto writer and
his maid. (We know what color she is.)
You, made of mud and expensive clay.
Given away, orphaned while your
parents lived, and ate, and breathed.
      What happens is this:
You grow and school. You train,
and there, finally, you are: a nurse,
prim in white, and there you are:
on your path, and there he is: a new
doctor, who may have worn a white coat,
or may not have (who is to say in this
construction?). What's important is
to say: you met, because you did,
married him and begat three girls
and the boy who would be king
(if you lived in the 19th century), but
you are in the 20th:
        formidable:
the dream of your own self, already
fixed to power: to the black country
doctor turning his black country (Haiti:
yes) into his own black country, and you,
like a pocket on his jacket, like a paquet
d'affaires. Like the key to the lock
to the room of gun-powder, of gold.
          O,
Simone Ovide Duvalier: don't let anyone
get in your way. Because you cannot be

a General, you become sinewy, broad,
ever-present. Throw the money you will
throw into the crowds in the town named
after you: Cité Simone. (You won't live
to see the slum it becomes, live to handle
the snake of danger hanging above each
doorway, live to see the black and brown
men who will scramble to rule after all
is done for you.)

You're as neat as a black dress with ribbons
and cinched waist. Imperious as its
shoulder pads. You: wife and mother
of dictators. You: A woman who has
everything to say, and finds a way
to say it.

Danielle Legros Georges

A CONGOLESE COTTON SHIRT EMBELLISHED WITH A PORTRAIT OF MOBUTU FROM THE COLLECTION OF THE TROPENMUSEUM IN AMSTERDAM

Mobutu: Your portrait sits atop a cotton field
of black, of spikes, gold and blood red,
embellished with the banner

L'homme du 24 Novembre. A sort of tomb
this shirt. Your mien more mean than not.
Who knows more than you?

Who vanquished his enemies more than you?
Your '65 surprise coup. Now you're the cover
for the body of a man

whose beating heart can enlivenyour face. Once
you beat, beat. The Belgians could not fix you,
the Americans were your friends.

You played them all. But the Dutch have you
locked in a case as a shirt made first
to do what?

Praise shirt. Shirt of glory. Shirt nonpareil.
God shirt. (Shirt of museum
capture.) Great god:

The trinity of you, atop a vivid cotton shirt.
L'unificateur. Unironic, you, look out
onto the world.

SOUL BONE

The rabbis say it lives
in a diamond-sized nubbin
at the base of the spine,

the static-puff hum
that haunts when it leaves,
makes us more

than mushrooms: curled
into a cabochon of bone
fashioned by the same mind

that made the Io moth without
a mouth, so it starves out
its brief week of life,

frantic for sex. Lacking
the pearl-string of a backbone,
where does the Io keep

its soul? Hard gem dropped
by a distracted lapidary
as ignorant of love

as the moth we named
for another god's lover, a priestess,
the one the stories say

he turned into a cow.

Lisa Rosinsky

DESERT

*"...the real invisible line separating chaos from order is not
the Strip at all but the parameter of the town dividing
Las Vegas from the desert, the landscape of spiritual
imagination, birthplace of three of the world's major
religions."*
        Mary Ruefle, "On Theme," Madness, Rack & Honey

What is it about the desert
that spawns gods and gamblers?

The Aolian harp plays itself,
or the plectra of the breeze do;
something in the sound sieves gods, maybe.

And gamblers are what's left.
Every grain of sand sings a fable:

agate on the tongue is said
to quench thirst. On the forehead,
it cures fever. The same stone

around the neck averts a lie.
So then how to tell the gods

and gamblers apart? By how much
light passes through them.
One's translucent; one's opaque.

Any dune might be divine,
but that's the risk you take.

Lisa Rosinsky

MOONRISE OVER HERNANDEZ

after the photograph by Ansel Adams

Daddy was driving so fast the clouds
galloped like movie cowboys

over red hills gone bloody
in the dying November sun,

when gravel flew and the car
skidded like a spooked horse—

wrangling his camera, Daddy
hollered at the men, at me,

the light meter, where's
the goddamn light meter, the light's
going,

and I watched him mutter
about foot-candles, slide film,

cock the shutter. He said he got it
and we got back in the car

and went home.
               Only after
the water-bath of these slick

years do I see it, the image
as he saw then: crosses,

chalk cloud, yawning
sky and dry skull of the moon.

Lisa Rosinsky

How unlikely any of it was.
Those precious seconds before

he took the shot, how the sun
left right after. That moment

of creation. How unlikely
that I was there, am here,

and here, and here.

LEAK

Without inspection
it looks fine!

everything

Take up space

GAME
GAME
GAME

PLAY
PLAY
PLAY

Take the time to
Take tender time
To take the tender
Moment of the time
More tenderized

In nature
In the fog
Movie it along
The challenging
But finding yourself
Is easy in the swift
Movement of surrender
Don't turn
Say goodbye but welcome

Raquel Balboni

Trust in the magic scene
Nothing very much makes sense
Who do I want to be there it is
Plainly

but don't even care to see
Just doing it all and screaming
Slowly from the swinging field
The windows without curtains

Nothing will ever make perfect sense
So don't cling to one
Live freely

How to say it all
blood
Meat blood

We have dinner ready

A glass of wine
A spliff or two
Drags of smokeables
Outtakes

I don't feel desolate
I don't feel out
Of my mind
Here in new faucet new beer new bed unforgettable rolling off the porch
Into untroubled waters, neutral
Face is so normal can't be anything else

Come off as harsh even if I'm friendly

LUNA MOTH
SUMMER SOLSTICE

Raquel Balboni

Calling time around midnight
Pheromones released
Green motion chair in the dark

Boiled alive

Freeeeeedom

It could be understood

Toon ears

Release

The spliffs the routine
Over and over again
You want me to send you new writing i don't know if i can

Raquel Balboni

COME

How people get along
Thrown in with the wolves
Waking up to easy coffee
How to keep on loving someone

Someone who thinks they are ugly but are very pretty

Oh great i did use the green heart
Getting it back
Maybe it was just a decision after all
To head back to the frontal base

Now all i need to do is figure out how to play music
So you see me from your window

There was no pre-noise

You don't have to feel rejected since the world is so big
Since so much can happen in a time well spent
Phone calls in the lawn a sad one over the grass someone died today
Friend in blue drowning the auburn stream to turn down the light

Sounds of coming
Charging all of my devices including my brain
The new memories bursting in when does a time become a memory?
How long after the moment dies can some voice hole say it is memory
Oh this memory so sweet so soft so delightfully horrifying a gasp that sounds
Demonic in pain from the yelping of automatic mouth, agape

Using the wand in public spaces
Masturbating in the library
The library truly makes me horny

Raquel Balboni

So what turns you on and how can i do it
Also make me cum i wish
Do it all again for another chance
To see how you make me come

Your attitude turns me on
Fantasy waves

A vibrator that is a necklace/ ring
Flex fits period cups

I usually think about this person most of the time but not intentionally in
this new way that has been brought out in the open.

What a treat it is walking by the donuts
The news the other lover
Sweet pumpkin the black fur lined fires
In the aisles a springing with colorful fulfillment
To get a grip on the box and lick it for what it's worth
Untimely effort to satisfy desires and then adapt new desires and fantasies
and use more time to fulfill new needs
Confronting the desires where is the end part the not very in public part
beginning to form in our mind box hovering between us next to the grass
and the street on the church side. We're here with so much in the way.

Strange it is very much so
Unusually obvious but insane
Can't get over the quivering
Next to the river next to the toilet on my knees in the bed
Strange it seems to become so in touch with the straight edge sword of
attraction. The purity rings a bell in the meadows of my mind with a long
haired white stallion trotting towards me like I'm watching it in a movie in
the front row with my eyes opened wide.

You can always say at least I didn't die

People are outside having fun i am inside having fun

Really comes down to wanting what you want and accepting
that

What what i done to deserve these thoughts
Will i want to engage in the fantasies i have made
Sexy ones with the older goblin in the wood cabin
The girl with small bones and amazing teeth
A big mouth i want to lick her all over

The freedom of it all the freedom of not thinking about it

Love listening to people come

It really just is like licky my pussy

We are all here with bodies that can come

Pleasure

I want to go with you somewhere

I feel like women may love each other anywhere

There love is everywhere, universally

Conclusion of spaghetti morning

Sexually happy there is no other way than the way the
pleasure hits and if you spread it openly
Now there is more time to come more time to seek horror
The way the mirror dances when the left hit gets out of line

Selfie art right now

THE NIGHT WITCHES

The Germans called us "Nachthexen";
they said our planes scratched the sky like sweeping
brooms as we passed. It was Hitler's way
of keeping us domestic, though later he swore
we were superhuman: fed on stealth injections
with eyes that burned the night like a cat's.

We were ghosts in the sky, gliding
on the night. Our brooms: canvas slung over
plywood. Parachutes, radios, defense ammunition,
all too heavy, our nocturnal ritual was made
with pencils, paper, a flashlight beaming
code to our comrades under the moon.

"Be proud you are a woman," we chanted
as we flew in formations of threes: two distracted
enemy planes, one dropped smooth, metal bombs,
eggs tucked up under our frostbitten wings.
In the night air, our light
wooden bodies flew free.

Perhaps after the war, we would not be asked to join a parade.
Perhaps after the war, we would go back to sewing, to our half-
families.

But during those nights, the air broke our skins, baptized us magic.

---

*The Night Witches, or the 588th Night Bomber Regiment, were the all female aviator
regiment of the Soviet Air Forces during World War II. Aged 17-26, they were crucial
assets to winning the war, dropping more than 23,000 tons of bombs on Nazi forces at
night. The 588th were not invited to the military parade celebrating victory, though they
were the most decorated unit of the Soviet Air Force.

THE BARN PIGEONS

My life began and ended in that barn,
not in the way you are thinking:

it was nothing to do with anger of father, indifference of step-
mother
it was nothing to do with the sting of a slap

But pear nectar, yes
Coo of pigeon

It was everything featherwing bluegrey the sharp press
of a peck on my skin, no blood drawn but all taken

*

Alice brought cold chicken and pie, fat greasing our lips
We spoke of the promise of flight and locked doors

How full of sun we could be when alone together, how we flew
into the softness of what we could share

My pigeons listened sighed settled their hollow boned bodies,
petticoated their feathers over open cracks to keep out light ears
the world

But step-mother, jealous mockingbird stealing eggs from another's
nest,
sang of Alice's come and go and dawn fell on softness in that
feather dark

Never leave your softness in the light, it will be found
Never leave your love unprotected, it will be caught

Pigeons are loyal creatures that always come home
Even when what greets them is an ax

Daughters are loyal creatures who always come home
even when what greet them are betrayals:

"I cannot take the whispers, we will be ruined."
And among these torn feathers of paper, the bones

and flesh and blood of beautiful love beheaded
and thrown in a barrel and sealed as if they were a dirty secret.

Daughters are loyal creatures but who will defend the poor birds?
Why do fathers kill what their daughter's love?

What have daughters to do but protect their own light?

---

*In 1892, Lizzie Borden was the first woman in the United States to be indicted for murder (her father and step-mother were killed in their home with a hatchet or ax). Rumors suggest that Lizzie was a lesbian, and that days before the murder, her father slaughtered her beloved pigions which she kept in the barn behind the house.

AUNTIE

When police arrived, she hovered
just beneath the ceiling,
her *oh* and *no* struggling to rise.

I don't believe she taunted him,
waving an apron as if at a bull:
"Old man, you can't even shoot straight."

Forty-six years they had teetered,
nearing the edge of a slide.

Did silence scream, one last time,
nagging the spouse neither
wanted or loved?

Or did she slump as he wavered:
his *oh* so soft and hideous
that only their tabby,
in the rafters, had any
chance to survive.

Elizabeth Lund

THIS WILL COST YOU

Change, change, it's all
about change, says the bard
from his Common bench.

Change, change, I bet you
want change, he demands
of a sunburned vet.

Who's that staggering
home, he asks of a financier
wearing scuffed wingtips.

A siege of girls in thin
pink heels, white pants
preens like hungry egrets.

Change, change, it's all
about change, he sings
again, jostling the blues.

A wispy blonde, one
arm in a sling, opens
her tiny red mouth.

Change, change. I like
that tune. But how
much will it cost?

CROSSINGS

One blind man with a cane,
one woman in a car. Both
entered the crosswalk.

His cane swept back and
forth, fishing. The woman
swallowed it up.

The blind man crashed
into her bumper and swore.
Struck it once with his cane.

The woman wanted to leave
her car, and bow down
to the man's staff.

One blind man groped
as before. One
woman sat in her car.

SCRUBSONG, AN EVICTION

I was reduced to the minerals crystalized along my brow and in the contours of my temples and the creases of my eyelids. I dragged my corpse from the sun-drenched marsh and lapsed into a peat-muddled pocket of water. I sank up into the grass and crabs and eels and thought of every place I'd ever been or filtering the breeze for memories or combing the tide for thrills or combing the tide for love or staring into the sun or staring into the sun or gliding beneath a pond for orgins to pull myself along.

Charlie Steinberg

AFTER *CUTTING THE STONE* BY HIERONYMUS BOSCH

The room comes into focus
present becomes scene— vignette
a warm light emerging from the locus of her voice
"warming thoughts"
I see twirling, strobing carousels
of white in the periphery, my arms
dipping deeper and deeper into pixelation.
I'm certain this isn't death—
toeing the edge of reset.
Warming thoughts... like fire and end times,
like a caffeine panic. My ears whistle the score to a fever dream
and I think of twisting
a lobster's tail from its torso,
of exposing greenery,
of whittling.

60% of me is water—
I wonder what I would rejoin
were my tail twisted off.

It's as simple as come and go—
arrival/absence.
All this time we've mistaken a tide for some other fate.

DEPTH SOUNDING

I.
Warm in my crib
and the hallway lights paint
an incandescent slat of gold
across the ceiling
and walls, the door ajar.
Following the sounds of dishes
and the wet sink, moving up and out,
and the exotic
tingle of escape and pain—
the room turning
over as leaves in wind.

II.
The farmer's dog sings
as I break through the wall of thorns.
The field is blue-lighted under the mountain's
moon-shadows and damp
with the onset of milky way.
Thistle and wheat smear the blood
from my legs as I silently
cleave the pasture
and in a sort of drunkenness,
I stare at the eastern
range, far against the horizon,
until I am home.

III.
I park by the swamp
and run through the cedars till the sky
opens to the ocean—the water and the moon
in a bright nightlight.

Charlie Steinberg

My skin flashes with sweat and twilight
like the jellies that wash
up along tide's edge—the kinds that glow
green and blue when shaken.
I drop my clothes
in a pile of bladderwrack
and leave with what I've learned, pulsing
in dull green bioluminescence
as the cedars take me back.

SOUND & VISION

The sun rising coral sky
forty-seven degrees to shift
on the right corner. Sealed up
for an escort. Pigeons flap
a shadow on the moss colored
wall. Across Bent and Omega

This is the final rise of star
for this Roman annual
Dust ourselves for tomorrow

We will burn curses as the sky
loses luster again. Sink gold
shift rose, smoke,
lavender ilk

Some friendships were lost
over diagnoses and gained
through witchcraft. Little
heart beats arrhythmically
We've got skullcap and parsnips
passionflower, lions mane, and
black eyed peas for the troops
Peasantry has always served
my kind for the purpose
of blending in
Polarized snapshots
Wicked tongue hold

That which rises in the wind

DESIGN FOR FLYING

If we wake to clouds broken
in darkness could we survive
an honest blessing of bird song
and black coffee? Hours
when the others in our lives
have tapped out for comfort
Letters left piled and scattered
for neglect, the way the news
chimes in to break the heart
again. There are tantrums
in the house. An avalanche
flood, thunder. We succumb
to going deaf. Wilt. Then
marched foot and clenched fist
provide dinner. The noise inside
the head that gets repeated on end
How it plays out. Your role
My role. Conversations we forget
to have. It is blindness that crushes
the throats of the young

PASSING AS THOUGHT

There's no specific way around
mortality as an absolute awareness
I'm unsure when exactly it started
motherhood, first diagnosis. They all fell
back to back. This life that I am responsible for when
there's little grip on this life that I am responsible for
Pragmatic conjectures lead one still round
to death. We fly. Jaywalk. Don't triple wash
our greens. Sleep in urban stacked sandwiched
wooden dwellings. Don't even get me started
on the shifting lands or the cyclone winds
Are things in order? What order is this we desire?
Can mine be a sing-a-long. A second line
Make room for me on the floor. In the bed
I'll keep the light on so you're sure. If I put
the thought into it now will it be better
for my return when we're alone? No matter what
you burn to the heavens I'll likely not go
as quietly as I've lived

THE UNREACHABLE IS ALWAYS WITH US

Our elders are taking leave
with many questions unanswered
Who will tell me
how to read the wind?
My tea leaves float in a pattern of rubbish
Visits in sleep go as cloudy lectures
mashed with Sunday graphics
to wake with indignity
I didn't get to write
We never talked
about Lilith or Nicomachus or scale

Orion and his little dog looking down
at my empty chamber

MARCH 23, 2017

for Joanne Kyger

How do you right a poem
when the sky is bursting forth
with radiant blue and
the clouds are formed
with that of a sculptor's hand
and somehow you, in your absence
from this earth, are everywhere
The sparrow bobs
The wind chime tones
The palms bend
And the news hammers
home that things are way
out of control

Allison Vanouse

FINESSE' IS FRENCH

finesse' is French. There are causes of language,
but other causes at a later period are also at work.
When a written literature, having its own good and expressive omission,
lying necessary and without distinction on the

>	veritable kitchen
>	table of integers

is imposing their languages merely onto two slightly different appropriations

>	1. 'succus', for amber
>	2. 'esteem', from abroad

we find that that is how it *always* is in England. Oftentimes luxuries
rather than necessities look goodly and expressive
from the ambiguous citizenship of their first proposer.
For instance, the Latin, having its own import--these are enough.
As a single illustration of the various quarters from which the existing

>	words are adjusted
>	these are a language.

They enumerate the various candidates for admission
from a sufficiently different *foyer*. So our dialectic
became, to beat embarrassment, farce.

Allison Vanouse

COMPELLED TO ADOPT THE LANGUAGE OF THE CONQUERED

compelled to adopt the language of the conquered
or after a while that which may be called a *transaction*:
there are causes for the existence of synonyms, reaching back
far into the history of a nation—here to possess
its own idiom: fire for the hearth.

One word for one word. The same, thus, in Greek
were originally elect in the midst of their differences—nay,
being few in number (both in forms sufficiently different
for the quintessential surrealist encounter) they were found
in feeling of processes very different from, much less formal-cum-
religious, acceptable forms of the same thing. Various tribes
each with its own dialect, having fixed themselves into one people.

This latter class, which are originally themselves (being but few in number),
                    find themselves
compelled at last to name that season "autumn"

like, *spring*.

Michael Schermerhorn

IN THE 1996 FILM *TWISTER*, HELEN HUNT WEARS A WHITE TANK TOP

And so the credits roll and we weep.
Not for the death of a father, the love story,
or the leveled drive-in featuring Jack Nicholson's
axe and Shelly Duvall's scarlet face.
But for our Oklahoma, the savaged trail
from Springfield to Worcester. It was as if
someone had folded a world map to let the belly
of the Midwest press itself against the cheek
of the Northeast. Crushed the hydrangea plants flat
in the crease. After the twister, everything had
a certain glow to it. Our house a swollen
monster. A cicada that swallowed the sun.
The sky yellow like mustard seed or saffron.
Up to our knees in light, every type of it.
The days lasting all night; the tourists photographing
the damage. Because the damage—
Some of the most astounding sculpture I'd ever seen.
My mother thought differently. In the aftermath,
she peered through the mist then grabbed
the broomstick, worked to brush the pine needles into a small pile,
choked on the vapor rising from the driveway toward
that stark sky. And later that night she must
have thought of the birds and the bugs
because I heard her muffled sobs stuffed
into the hay-filled mattress on the daybed in a neighbor's basement,
a home while ours unbuilt.
She cleaned like that even before the storm:
on Sundays, about once a month. Sweating
through a white tank top,
rewarding herself with a vodka
on ice like all
heroes do.

185

KINMEDAI

"Iridescent," we called it. The way it splayed with its sheath exposed. Not beet red but ruby, a microscopic tide pool for an eye. We started there: pulled the golden-socket pearl for our scalloped tongues. Then, running the pointed end of the wooden chopstick down its collar, extracted the meat from its bones as though we were debriding a burn wound. Careful, with a subtle violence. Every tug, every smack of the lip—the fish's mouth petrified and agape, stuck in something like wonder or consternation. Perhaps had we shown some mercy, we would be left with something more than a pile of scale and fin. But here is the secret: we used our hands, practiced vigilance. Moving in small, swift motions so as not to disrupt this divine face staring back at us, however eyeless. And so it goes—

This: my witching hour. And this: abundant joy.

Michael Schermerhorn

BELIEVE

The whole of this would carry more drama
were I to say that I mistook the parade float ascending the corner
for my grandmother's off-gold sedan,
though that would be inaccurate; she
hasn't driven in years on account of her dementia.

Standing at the corner of Boylston and Clarendon:
me—the taste of grapefruit, a head above the crowd—
straining for a glimpse at the pickup truck carrying the tempo
along the path of denim shorts, rainbow plastic beads—
This dude just grabbed my ass and I liked it but fuck him.

I'm not crying because of the guy's callused
hand that made a noise when he dragged it across
the seat of my pants but because I know every word
to the Cher song blazing through the portable speakers
perched atop the rear window of the pickup.

Track one on *The Very Best of Cher*,
the staple record of my grandmother's Toyota.
Alongside her and my brother, I learned the words to every line
as we drove to the pizza place with the good salad dressing
down Valatie on the way to my little cousins' house.

I am surprised I remember all of this,
even now—piss drunk and street-level.
It has been more than a decade. I have—what have I done?—
learned what it means to taste the inside of men,
found hair in places I didn't know to explore—

In other words, I have grown into something I am still
trying to manage.

This past April, my father had to introduce me to his mother.
No more Toyota, no more records—she refused to take her medication,
and I have become a stranger in the interim. I wonder
what she would say to all this color. I wonder how many times
I'd have to tell her about the men in my life for her to recall

the always changing shape of my queerness. I wonder if she would be
        proud too.

MISERY

after Bianca Stone

Somewhere, like liberty, I am grinding my head
through a washboard and collecting the debris.
You are hiding in the kitchen,
you are pushing ice cubes from the silicone tray.
Of course I've a beer in hand,
a pocket of yeast collecting at the bottom like the dunes
in the desert feature on BBC One.
You notice my knack for details.
You notice my hand on your thigh,
and of course that's an excuse for a hangover.
I think of you asking *how are you doing*
one million two hundred ninety six thousand
six hundred and eight times a day,
and how I always think to half-joke
suffering,
and you laugh every time.
You make sure I fail to note the misery in that.
I make sure to note my own hyperbole.
What I am trying to say is that we existed
worlds apart but never cared to notice.
What I am actually saying is that I did love you then,
but now I'm speculating again,
and I almost forget your middle name.
Together, we are a gruff man leaning hard
with his hip against the hood of a pickup truck,
the sunshine feeling more like sand
coating our swollen throat.
It's days like this you tell me about your fear
of the word *different*,
how waking up next to another man
feels more like a handful of holy dirt

Michael Schermerhorn

thrown over your moonglow forehead.
On the hood of the pickup,
or inside and draped across the upholstered seat covers,
I tell you my vision of heaven:
a world where we are caked in light
and coffee grounds
and straight men are relegated
to the pleather-stitched booths at the rear
of an Outback Steakhouse.
Our skin is clear. You are looking like a hero.
You are a dog and I am too, sometimes.
Since we are in heaven we no longer require bladders.
And since we are in heaven we don't have to mourn like this.

SCULPTING

almost there
/ must revert /

burgle the

memory-
museum /

find relevance

within
retrograde /

among

the clutter
/ must identify

the keynote

[brain-sigh \ fix-cage \\

              a jaundiced brick-built \\

                              voice-
condom\\

      baton \\

            always something after us \\

ghosting \

star-gazer\\

a curtain \ elsewhere-fuse\\

faded 8-track tape \\

salami & licorice \\

mustard-colored leaves\ gold-colored grass\

the scarecrow\\

steel bucket \ woodstove ashes \ water \\

a squall]

the squalls
also theirs /

before these

beginnings
a bang /

and then you

began
to take form

Kevin McLellan

AT LEAST FOR NOW

told an attentive stranger that

the magic's gone / you meant
allure / then the circling refrain

/ "this could be the last time

I..." / your mind a playground
merry-go-round / a flash / a blip

/ then an ascending plane / try

your impatient hand / must
refrain from furthering goodbyes

Kevin McLellan

MENAGERIE

you wait for forecasted hail

to ping / against windows
/ windows aren't merely

memories / you take an umbrella

for a walk while one-hand
texting /notice an acquaintance

in the distance / per usual he

uses excuses / takes shortcuts /
tells you he lost this weight

from a meat-only diet / yes /

you're sad that the animals
will be angry in his heart

Kevin McLellan

THE BOXER

identify the language
of his steps / usually

in the crease of their

departure / birth
defect or frost or dog

bite / you attempted

to not look at the top
of his missing ear / then

into you his leaning

and you ask, do you feel
a part of or apart?

Kevin McLellan

A STORM

Tired of of / tired
by by / your here-

fuse shortening / by

no means explosive
nor in need of a voice-

condom / meanwhile

elsewhere / you're
not unlike a ballast

Meg Tyler

BUSHMILLS, NORTHERN IRELAND

Swallows surround the gables, an airy havoc.
    Although autumn, the brightness of day
        lingered into evening. I remember when
            the slender dark shapes flitted past
                the window, as if another form
                        of consciousness were trying
    to get through. Unseen to us
were the ruminative cows, the clouds
    flying past above the mountain.
            Enlarged at first, did our love, after all,
                become focused and insistent
                    like the needs of small children. Before the birds
                        went south, before the cows arrived at the abattoir.

THE ART OF THE TROUBLES

The Ulster Museum, Belfast, 2014

The first thing I saw
      was a woman blown high
            by a blast. An iron cast.
Then, to the left, an open

      mouth, the colors smeared,
            the no sound that came out, receding but registered by
Le Brocquy, whose brush

      insists on features
            that peel away
                  and remove the self
to another shore of

      being. In the next room,
            an abandoned island,
            segmented by crumbling
stone walls. Gerard Dillon's house.

      Three donkeys, painted sheep.
            The waves blue and quiet,
                 not crashing, the only
sound from an outboard motor

      of the two men on their way.

FREQUENCY

The clematis vines into its top knot of magenta,
       each petal as bold as the arm of a starfish.
My child puts down his bow and strokes
       the white keys of the piano as his violin
teacher opens the hutch to feed Attila the Bun.
       The flowers of the mimosa tree
color the air like the notes she will teach him
       to play: E, F, C sharp. Her gentle alertness
to my son's shifting gaze and sudden movements
       from instrument to instrument is captured by
the bunny's delicate awareness, registered
       in his whiskers, which are as long as his body is wide.
Sympathetic vibrations, she says.
       The conversations between them:
A to D string, teacher to child, the sound
       waves that keep us tuned and in tune.

LATE JUNE

Heralds the long-awaited eruption: hemerocallis,
clematis and astilbe spill over the brick walkway.
Meanwhile, the body exercises to its own clock.
New growths arrive: spur of bone, lipoma, calculi.

The body succumbs to the challenge.
But the mind, like a cormorant on top of the dead
cottonwood: prescient, supple, swift, targeted.
Unlike most things human, forgiving, forgiven.

OF COLOR

Looking down from above, the lens
      picks up wildflowers in the foreground,
      their varieties of astonishment.

Striated red-brown cliffs give over
      to the white mouth of the beach
      where the waters come to feed.

Here lives a balance that the landscape, like love,
      does not design but achieves.
      As bone-white sand meets azure sea,

dun pebble against soot-colored slate. Above,
      stone frames the clover-colored glass
      in a church window and

turquoise tile tops an earthen grave.

THE SHAWL

> *"Everything of which we become*
> *conscious...causes nothing"*
> *Nietzsche*

On a lucky day, I wear settledness around me
like a shawl knit by your mother in Chennai.
Sloping towards the lake, the garden gives over
its colors to summer. Greens rush toward the water's edge,

then stop. Twitters, buzzing, croaks.

Meg Tyler

HIS FIRST CONCERT

An unfashionable group assembles
      on the floor for Bach, Philip Glass.
Bows cut the air, vertically. The cellists chin their chests,
      like boxers. Crescendo, diminuendo,
pizzicato. Wafting towards us from a deep bank by the stage
      was the scent of hundreds of red roses
in their finite but ecstatic blooming.

TÚ, PADRE BAUDELAIRE

París

Entrando por la rue Auguste-Comte
y atravesando por el Jardin du Luxembourg
para llegar al Boulevard du Montparnasse,
di con la visión de frondosos árboles en su verde,
verdadero verde,
y tres espléndidas explanadas.
El verde siempre invita a reposarse
sobre la alfombra, naturalmente, recibir el sol,
hacer yoga, picnics...
y que los niños jueguen a sus juegos.

Soleado día de julio—y mis pies llevaban prisa.
Por el blanco sendero sembrado de guijarros
doblé a la izquierda
y puesto que tu cuerpo, padre Baudelaire,
ha estado ausente de la tierra,
verte allí de pronto hecho piedra permanente,
tu busto en alto para toda la eternidad,
¿cómo no detener mis pasos, elevar la frente
para contemplarte?
Una llamarada verde de árboles era el horizonte
detrás de ti—verdosas densidades a lo Delacroix.
Enseguida te di las gracias y más gracias
por haberme en estos años alumbrado cuando
a mi ventana le faltaba luz,
cuando una y otra vez las palabras me eludían
y la absurda y alta luna
francamente me aburría.

Si bien ya no recorres las calles
ni los salones literarios de esta metrópoli viviente,

seguiré tus pasos adonde me lleven y, un día,
cuando me acerque un tantito a tu estatura,
y estén los árboles reverdeciendo, vendré a verte.
Sin tropezarme demasiado con mis versos
en *la hermosa lengua de mi siglo,*
vendré con ganas a decirte lo que he visto,
a contarte cómo aquí en la tierra siguen las cosas.

YOU, FATHER BAUDELAIRE

Paris

Crossing le Jardin du Luxembourg
from Rue Auguste-Comte,
bound for Boulevard du Montparnasse,
I came face-to-face with a vision of leafy trees in all of their greenness,
so deeply green,
and three splendid esplanades.
Greens are an open invitation to lie back, naturally,
on a carpet of grass and bask in the sun,
to practice yoga, picnic...
and let children play at their games.

A sunny day in July—and my feet were moving fast.
Down a white path sown with pebbles,
I turned left, when,
knowing your body has long been gone from this earth,
Father Baudelaire, I saw you suddenly immortalized in stone,
your bust raised up for all eternity:
how not to stop in my tracks, not lift my countenance
to dwell on you?
You stood against a green conflagration of trees
lining the horizon—dense and verdant like a Delacroix.
I hastened to thank you again and again
for the years you gave me light
when at my window there was none,
for the times when words escaped me,
and the moon looked so lofty and absurd,
I confess I was bored.

You no longer frequent these streets
or the literary salons of this vibrant city, but still

I will follow your footsteps wherever they lead me, and someday,
aspiring to even a fraction of your stature,
when trees are greening-up again, I will come to you.
Without stumbling too clumsily over my own verses,
in *the beauty of the language of my century,*
I will come to you longing to say what I have seen,
to explain how things have been going here on earth.

Translated by Lisa Horowitz

*Once I thought I had found
the Metaphysical Substance.*

GOLD

after John Ashbery

Here we go again.
Barely tolerated

& living on the margins—
pollen sinking in a breeze,

popular & peopled like a sneeze,
the returning ones

like a cloud dreaming,
like an old joke retold.

Suffering the glow
of growing dull.

Don't you wonder why
through all this—
giving way to elbows & tears—

corruption survives, hell
thrives—and models
everything on old deals.

Tomorrow they say
will be purer, more radiant

& we will soar higher
on stolen wings.

THE SMALL HOURS

The angle
of shadow

upon your
earthly thigh,

that bristling
near-white,

follicles that raise
themselves

when I touch
the back of your hand—

a primordial creature
responding

to a brief change
in water temperature, a

glistening of light
on a still

water surface, deep
in the metaphor

of unearthly
love.

Marc Vincenz

Is it just that I yearn
for a gentle immersion?

A BREW

Concocted where love was
        just yesterday.
Vague to me, yet
        an image made
in a hotel room.
        That form of days
turned into years.
        The end, so it began.

Don't say anything at all.

Simply watch the outline
        of the trees
& the clouds restlessly
        clutching the cold light.

ONE MAN'S NORTHAMPTON

for JH

No matter what, gallant.
A word he rubbed
Between his hands
To keep warmer.
So, he says, *tell me.*
Now you know
What it's like to die,
How does it really feel?
In times like these the voice
Fails. A crackle. Still twisting
The dial—the way we once
Tuned in and out.
To die or to be dead?
Not yet, I say, hands behind
My back contemplating
And complaining to them-
Selves. A grumble.
As he applauds me,
The cigarette just lit
Falls from his lips. The ash
Burns a hole in his shirt.
Meanwhile, above, the sky
All dark clouds, gathers
Itself to wait out the night.
Somehow it floats
More Easily by.

FOREWARNING

From the myth
which has no end
but is always transforming.

From the theft of fire
to the pursuit of a loved one
in the city of the dead, the

salvation from the flood
or the deep search for eternal
life where we are surrounded

by ourselves rather than the world—
missing the patterns
of thought behind words.

From this unlighted cabin
window, the air unhooks itself
and darts away.

SILENT PRAYER

for A

How could I expect you
to climb out of your grave

& creep through
your old haunts,

to stand beside me
& point out who walks

like a martyr &
who walks like a rose?

Your millions set adrift
in conveys headed

to the edge of death,
the moon above

& below, quantum
illusions, figurative

or literal expressions
of what is to come

& who is to haunt us—
winding down the track—

a countryside path
taken by all those countless souls.

How bitter the taste of this breeze.

A TRIP TO THE MOON

Mortality a faint whisper, a life permanent ...

Moonless in thought, tidal though,
To unfield the even pasture, newly

Hewn to an old man's stubble.
The greys, the insolent weeds unwinding

The threat of what wants to be bread
Or corn, the lost cattle, stymied, the rest

Wishing to be forlorn, to be missing out
Like the crone inside the daft hut, raised

Above the hills, with the last glass of wine—
Heady but headed backward into, into

The motion, uneven and solitary, quivering
Into latter days or trains ricketing, crickets

Hopscotching, clambering deep into,
Deep into the roots, underearth into, into

The lost time of anywhere, of adventure,
Of jungle spirit, of subsumed, then en-

Raptured, until more greys, discovering
This planet in a lucky commotion, a crackling

Of static, that background radiation, a thought
From the beginning of time. Here we stand, caught adrift,

Planting flags, clutching at straws, to forget
All bets and land seamlessly on the face of a cartoon.

Here in the islands,
no bold proposals or
the hissing frenzy of afternoons
and evenings in the metropolis.

AMONG THE MACHINES OF VIRTUE & VICE

Dare I say, the labyrinth was in her mind,
the path memorized like those choral verses
she had known from childhood.

She glanced down toward the assembled,
hoping somehow, she too might impart
what she knew. A lifetime

had taught her a little less than half
& it reflected in her laughter, which
was strained at best. She imagined

him as a lighthouse in a maelstrom
of cross-currents, of unpredictable shallows
—it was pure tomfoolery,

of course, thinking of her own symbolic
discoveries as, too, the illuminations—
a faint roar that murmured deep

in her inner ear that seemed to say
something wants to be known.
To her, though, words meant little anymore.

Electric through, the channels of runoff
that twist through the once-primordial forest,
& the smoke emerging from funnels

spilling out words on the sky: Please don't die.

Calm consideration requires just the margins
of a newspaper something dragged under

the noses of authorities in their paralyzing
pinstripes. Who lectures on death anyway?
It's all about the dying or those stasis chambers

frozen cryogenic in the chorus
of the patriarch, the wind that bellows
in its incontinent rain or sister snail

in her slow skate across the melting ice
of uneven waters. *Present is this island,*
the cracking face of a perpetual cold.

We remember her still, even through
all the dark clouds in her ancient tiles
when people were carried by a wave

through their generous ghettos
& found their fates along the barriers
of truth. Could we walk along

the alleys singing, waving our masks
among the machines of virtue & vice,
spreading our salt fondly

where we all walk intrepid in a curved space.
Eventually, the cold will hit her eyes, &
just for a second, she shall see

her other face boldly clearing
the way down to the waterfront.

> *Foliage and forest, the heart of the land;*
> *silence and sentience, the soul of the sea.*

Kim Garcia

FOG SHRINKS THE WORLD TO THIS ROOM

where Donne found love enough, and playful wit. I am
timid and distractible, twitching at every twit, flinching
when wind slams the door. What am I afraid of? Habits

of mind, we, but I feed that nervous creature. A neon buoy
is just visible in the pause that blots out view. A rubber bulb
of air with a pierced nipple where a fraying line tethers it

to some deeper drama—a rock forcing current against itself,
with treacherous collision, a cage, a baited hook. Death at play.
On the bulge of water the moon draws up, winds urge yet more

water on water. Lavish. And dangerous, as the good things are
too often, for my timid self, who always asks, like a child
on a car trip, "But how long until?" and "How will this end?"

Kim Garcia

THE WINDOW

in fog is a square of gray, blank canvas, cream from a sorrowful cow.
The foghorn lows mournfully, what else? Clytemnestra. No one listens,

and she's always right. Exhausting to know so much dull information,
useless until it finds its listener. Inert. This morning I walked an empty

wharf before the sun was up. A hungry gull looked me over as meat,
in beak-sized chunks, assessed my empty hands, considered my utility

from every angle—parts, conveyer, carrion—found nothing of interest.
It is easy to make peace with such appraisals, delivered without rancor.

Even the unseen hands of capital and human carelessness don't carry
the shiv of language, of words crafted to enter the body just so, angled

to miss bone and find that intimate organ, faithful as weather, beating.
Wonder also fissures along such paths, lightning through sand, fingers

of glass left of the flood. It hasn't been written what this day shall be.
Field birds counterpoint the tide as it sounds the rocks. Let me be

                        the praising creature,
the one who mourns the extinction of a single wave. Let me have a use.

SUMMER POEM

Beethoven's sonatas, news of our daughter's engagement,
sunlight, a shower overlooking water—the good things
of life, which must bulk up with shadow to be seen round.

A red squirrel carries twine in its mouth—a sure sign
of a nest under the house, new life seeking its way
into the walls, through fiberglass bedding salted by waves

blown beyond shape, a scarf unfurling, over the field
and against the windows. It works its way in everywhere,
the jade-green winter sea. How beautiful the destruction.

A deaf man may fashion music from memory, baby squirrels
bring their own babies to nest in the pink plush. Durable
where destruction sets its fire, flood, unforgivable wrong.

What do we call "evil" today? The ravens are playing
in the storm. Only a broken heart says, "Nevermore."

Kim Garcia

THE DESK AT LONGVIEW

A field of uneven ground, meadow grass
with seed heads of rust and crimson, scrub,

wind off the water catching each, but answered
with a different dance, a shiver of movement

or muscled roll. Wind chimes ring loco here,
and the surface of the incoming tide twitches

with cross currents, mediating above and below.
But the foghorn presides, as though it brought word

from a deep-dug well of gray distance, always present.
An Om. Not kind, not unkind.

BREEZES NORTHWESTERLY

       The whine of a saw over wave-crumple, a load
of timber being tumbled far off, or the rattle
of a truck on a patch of uneven road, a shudder,
then relief.
                Even dying animals rest between
gasps. A bitch birthing her pups stops to lick
each face clean before the work of the next. We live
in anxious times, tweet and blur, without touch.

       Today a stiff breeze blows down from the Yukon,
from the melting Arctic, a continent of implacable white,
where once men died to plant a flag, locate latitude, calculate,
precise about it. Now slush tankers churn pale blue.

             Shut the windows, and you're still amongst it:
Life rushing the windows, Life looking solemnly on, Life
writing these words, reading them, setting the book aside, taking
it up. Where is the line, the latitude, the end I'm fearing? And then?

Kim Garcia

WHAT IF

What if this is a mistake? Another place where I let things force in
because I can't tell gift from bribe, a trick? Or where I get in the habit

of sniffing and circling until there's nothing left but wariness, tigers
circling their tree until they become butter? What if this morning's

blue cove, with its pooling calms of clashing current, canceling surface
tensions, glassing over with the look of a still pond, what if

something impossible were about to happen, something impossibly good?
Who is at home to catch it? To finger the filigree? To say,

without reservation or reserve, with an excess of hope, "It's perfect."
It is a brink worth teetering on—this delight, this disaster.

ESSAYS

GERRIT LANSING'S TRANSITIONS

I.

  In April and May of 2017 I taught a six-week seminar
on Charles Olson and his Black Mountain and New American
contemporaries at the Maud / Olson Library in East Gloucester,
a two-room space holding volumes collected by professor Ralph
Maud, titles Olson is known to have read, owned, or been loaned,
in effect a facsimile of Olson's life of reading; seated at Olson's own
plywood tressle table, views of Gloucester Harbor out the windows,
we discussed Olson in conjunction with Robert Creeley, Hilda
Morley, John Wieners, Robert Duncan, Stephen Jonas, Edward
Marshall, Nathaniel Mackey, Fred Buck, and Gerrit Lansing.
Gerrit, to my surprise, although I should've known better, attended
the classes, all six. His health was declining, that was clear, but all
the way through he maintained the sublime patience and impish
humor he was known and admired for. When the week arrived
for our class to study him, Gerrit good naturedly recited his own
work in the round tones of his precise, oratorical diction, including
"Abbadia Mare," a nod to our shared connection to Hammond
Castle, where Gerrit lived as a guest of inventor and radio control
innovator Jack Hammond, and where I, a high school senior and
college freshman, worked as a tour guide thirty years later.
  I first met Gerrit at his bookstore Abraxas on Main Street
in Gloucester when I was thirteen, and Abraxas was soon to close;
the store's wooden sign, about four feet tall, was fixed to the
building, beckoning "Used Books," a painted hand extending an
index finger up to the second floor. I climbed the stairs, hearing
my own feet scuff the steps in the echoing stairwell, and entered
the single room constituting Abraxas: the place was crammed with
books set on two-by-fours elevated on cinder blocks, all the New
Age, paranormal, occult books, books on Ancient Egypt, the cheap
mass-market paperbacks: it was bewildering and exciting, a jumble
unlike any bookstore I'd been to, and my only frame of reference

for what I'd encountered was H.P. Lovecraft, which I discovered much later was not far off the mark.

When I returned to Gloucester from Cambridge in 2005 it was through Amanda Cook's good graces that I was invited to Gerrit's house on Western Avenue overlooking Stage Fort Park; soon I, too, was a fixture of Gerrit's living room gatherings, late-night talk amidst family heirlooms in glass cabinets, his large, ornate, fiery maple-looking piano, the two square coffee tables of blond wood pushed together to make a platform for piles of mail, library books, poetry pamphlets, and occult magazines, and, of course, the framed sketch of Gerrit drawn in the fifties by Jane Freilicher, a momento of his New York days.

Despite the friendship we shared, I was taken aback when he called me after our last Olson class on May 13 to ask if I would work with him to organize his papers and manuscripts, to serve, in his words, as his "literary executor" after his death. We worked together closely for the next nine months, separating letters, postcards, poem fragments, torn-out notebook pages, from bills, junk mail, obsolete calendars, old newspapers, moving the mountain one pebble at a time with the ultimate goal of amassing an archive that would serve as the companion and completion of the correspondence he'd already sold to Yale.

Yet as the months progressed, medical appointments proliferated, and his discomfort and neck pain grew more acute. In retrospect, I realize now how great his pain must've been, and the extent to which he masked it. It was only during his last two weeks that the direness of his condition became apparent.

During his last days, the house filled with friends maintaining a vigil. The piano was rolled across the living room, away from Western Avenue, so Gerrit could recline in a rented hospital bed facing the water, and east. He never shooed these grieving acquaintances away, although once I heard him weakly beg for quiet so he could sleep.

II.

Gerrit had been born on February 25, 1928 to Charles and Alice (Scott) Lansing, the youngest child, by far, of three. Older sister Alice was named for mother; brother Charles, for father. Then came baby brother Gerrit Yates Lansing, whose name originated with an ancestor (from whom it might be argued Gerrit inherited his distinctive eyes) who served three terms in the U.S. Congress, a stalwart of Albany's business life. Other ancestors included John Townsend, a mayor of Albany, and Ambrose Spencer, also a Congressman.

Gerrit's own father, who served during the First World War in Europe as an engineer, established himself as a dominating influence in Cleveland's industrial sector; he was invited onto the boards of non-profits, including Western Reserve University. Gerrit's mother, however, was born into an affluent Southern family that had relocated to Washington, D.C., and her close friend Constance (Pulitzer) Elmslie was known to Gerrit as "Aunt Constance."

The Lansings inhabited a sprawling estate in Chagrin Falls, Ohio, called Scotlan (*not* Scotland) Farm. An aerial photo shows not only a commodious Georgian-style colonial revival home, but many out-buildings, such as stables, a green house, houses for servants and guests. Gerrit once told me about his job on his father's gentleman's estate, decapitating chickens; when he held them upside down they lost consciousness, and the knife sliced easily.

He attended the Park School of Cleveland, a progressive middle school; the student magazine *Arrow* carried several of his poems that show so many of Gerrit's hallmarks, his playfulness and wit. After Park, he went to Bainbridge High, then Harvard. At Harvard, it's often said, Gerrit associated with John Ashbery, Frank O'Hara, and Edward Gorey; while true to a point, the most intimate friendship Gerrit had with a Harvard classmate was, from what I can tell, with John McGavern (both were 1949 graduates).

McGavern was also an aspiring poet, and later became director of the University of Hartford's library system. Not only do Gerrit's letters to McGavern survive (returned to Gerrit after McGavern's death), but Gerrit safeguarded McGavern's poetry manuscripts, all still unpublished. The McGavern letters, as well as Gerrit's letters to his mother from college and shortly thereafter, constitute a valuable cache of material to aid any future biographer of Gerrit's ideas and whereabouts during the late 1940s, early 1950s.

After graduating from Harvard, Gerrit got a job as an editorial assistant in New York, and looking through the books he owned I saw many had tell-tale pencil marks, Gerrit's corrections of punctuation, spelling. He pursued a master's degree at Columbia, too. And then Gerrit became enmeshed in the whirl of glamour and late-night carousing associated with Broadway lyricist John Latouche; he met Latouche's lover (or former lover), Harry Martin, a painter and World War II medical orderly who'd studied at St. John's College in Annapolis, Maryland, on the GI Bill. Kenward Elmslie, son of "Aunt Constance," became Latouche's partner, and the two bought a farmhouse together in Calais, Vermont. Gerrit became close with German emigree author Ruth Landshoff Yorck, composer Ben Weber, painter Ellsworth Kelly, and a circle of friends that included Howard Griffin, Joe Burns, Tom Cassidy, and an Alabama-born man going by the name of Jack Dempsey. The literary activity of this group was memorialized in Daisy Aldan's *Folder* (and, later, *A New Folder*) and in *Semi-Colon*, the poetry newsletter published by Tibor de Nagy Gallery. I was pleasantly surprised to discover that the details of Gerrit's scene – overshadowed in New York by the Beats, but existing on the fringe of Broadway as an analogue to Berman's activities in Los Angeles on the edges of Hollywood – were captured in minute detail by Patrick Balfour, 3rd Baron Kinross, in his 1959 travelogue *Innocents at Home* (publishing under "Lord Kinross"). Kinross described Gerrit as living in a "chronically disordered apartment" characterized by "a hookah and a pack of playing cards." When late-night conversation turned to "the Nature of Truth and the

Meaning of Life" Lord Kinross ducked out. Kinross lived with Harry Martin in Martin's cold water apartment on York Avenue up against East River Drive, following the Latouche group's reveries at haunts such as the Bon Soir cabaret, Lüchow's in the East Village, and the Baby Grand.

Even as Gerrit participated in the late-night, after-show Broadway demimonde, meeting (through Latouche) a host of luminaries like Dashiell Hammett, Marc Blitzstein, and W.E.B. DuBois, he began studying with (again, through introductions made by Latouche) occult practitioner and teacher Stefan Walewski, who claimed the title of Count Stefan Colonna-Walewski, author of a single volume entitled *A System of Caucasian Yoga*. Due to an introduction made by John Hays Hammond Jr. (yet another friendship brokered by Latouche), Gerrit began publishing with Eileen Garrett's Parapsychology Foundation. He also studied astrology with Maria Crummere and Zoltan Mason. However, as late as 1965 Gerrit was confessing in a letter to Oscar Weber that, although he had a basic or limited ability to erect a chart, "I have less proficiency in the interpretation of charts and am most often baffled by the problem of synthesis ... I am at a loss when it comes to interpretation, to say nothing of progressions or rectification." It's interesting to note how much of Gerrit's fluency with occult material dates to his later stay at Hammond Castle in Gloucester, as formative as the New York period undoubtedly was.

When John Latouche died in August of 1956 at his co-owned Calais farmhouse, Gerrit's social scene came under great strain: Harry Martin was the only one present when Latouche succumbed to thrombosis (later confirmed by autopsy), and it was his panicked order to the household servants to burn the bloody mattress Latouche died on that brought down on him the suspicion of Latouche's family. (Lord Kinross recounts all these details in *Innocents at Home*.) Gerrit and Harry Martin repaired to Gloucester, taking up residence in inventor Jack Hammond's granite castle on the coast of Magnolia in sight of Norman's Woe. From the castle they ventured out to Fort Square, a waterfront neighborhood of Italian immigrants where poet Charles Olson lived after shuttering Black Mountain College (I should note my own great-grandparents, immigrants from Milazzo, lived two buildings down from Olson when Gerrit and Harry Martin got up the courage to knock on Olson's door).

Although he'd first read Eliphas Levi's *Transcendental Magic* (A.E. Waite's translation) in 1945, perhaps as an incoming Harvard freshman, and Crowley as well, Gerrit threw himself into studying Western Esotericism at Hammond Castle and after Hammond's 1965 death while he continued to live in Gloucester. In New York, he'd identified primarily as Buddhist, cultivating non-attachment, but the nexus of activity at Hammond Castle seems to have acted as catalyst for Gerrit's commitment to, and enthusiasm for, Crowley's writings and thought. In 1961, when Gerrit published the first issue of his magazine *SET*, he included poems written by Crowley (already, by then, in the public domain) under the magical name Frater Perdurabo.

SET was Gerrit's calling card, not only in the poetry world, enabling him to reach out to Robert Duncan, Ed Dorn, or Diane Wakoski (the first issue of *SET* is one of the very few times John McGavern's poems saw print) but Gerrit also deployed it in occult circles, mailing the first issue unsolicited to Karl Germer, Aleister Crowley's literary executor and successor as Outer Head of the Ordo Templi Orientis (OTO). Germer, then approximately 75 years old, retired in California, exchanged several letters with Gerrit. In them, Germer comes across as initially suspicious, but ultimately professional and cool. He objected to Gerrit's title, since, in Germer's mind, the Egyptian god Set, the god of tumult and upheaval, represented all that was levelling and "Bolshevik," all that was wrong, so much so that in one sentence his language reached the boiling point.

But Gerrit caught flack from Olson too, who accused Gerrit in at least one letter of holding himself aloof in Romantic affectation from the messiness and commonness of reality. And when Gerrit sent poems to Olson's contacts in New York, to New

Directions, for instance, rejection slips inevitably showed up in the mailbox. He kept at it, publishing in the last issue of John Wieners' *Measure* (alongside James Schuyler, Barbara Guest, Duncan, Lamantia), and in John Sinclair's *Work*. In 1966, Joan and Robert Kelly's Matter Press imprint (distributed by Jim Lowell's Asphodel Bookshop in Cleveland) published Gerrit's first book, *The Heavenly Tree Grows Downward*, with a preface by Wieners. Some of Gerrit's "signature" poems – poems he remained proud of, performing and republishing throughout his life – appeared in this 1966 edition.

A third burst of enthusiasm in Gerrit's life from this time was for Deryk Burton, a sailor born in Wallasey, England, a mid-sized town on the western side of the Mersey River, who he met, as Brian King told me, at the Studio Restaurant on Gloucester's Rocky Neck. Known as Gerry and Derry to close friends, they rented a house in Annisquam, and sailed a client's yacht to its winter berth in Fort Lauderdale, Florida. For more than thirty years they stayed together, until Deryk passed away in 1997.

Gerrit's battle with alcoholism isn't a secret. Going into recovery was a profound, spiritual event for him, and for years he attended AA sessions. He'd been drinking heavily since his Latouche days when parties ended with the rising sun, but he'd weathered the loss of Latouche, and the crisis of the inquest and autopsy. Hammond died in 1965. In 1966, Ruth Yorck, a much closer friend, famously died of a heart attack in the arms of Ellen Stewart (founder of LaMama) at a performance of Peter Weiss's *Marat / Sade*. Olson died in January, 1970. Stephen Jonas, one month later. In Annapolis, he sold books alongside other dealers at Circle West, continued to add to *Heavenly Tree*, and made new friendships, but I can't help feeling his Annapolis period was one of relative isolation; it was there he hit bottom, and at the urging of his sister Alice, sought the help he required.

By 1982, Gerrit was back in Gloucester tending to Abraxas and living with Deryk in Magnolia, writing poems; poets in Boston were drawn to him, and his life and correspondence seems to blossom after his Gloucester return. When Alice passed away Gerrit closed Abraxas (in 1992) and bought the grand home perched above Stage Fort Park where I spent many hours with him, and where he hosted innumerable gatherings. His last 26 years were characterized by rising early, meditating, reading prodigiously, and writing when so moved (which was more and more often). Magnolia's verdure, and Gloucester's burgeoning literary scene, were a matrix of engagement that helped him maintain his formidable mental powers as time progressed.

III.

In May of 2018 I was brought back in by the personal representative appointed under Gerrit's will to gather, organize, and catalogue the components of this last half of Gerrit's archive. As of this May it'll be one year since then, two since I began working with Gerrit. I've been fishing important documents from all corners of the house, from piles on the floor, from old crates, checking his library of 20,000 books for tucked-in postcards; I've assembled it all into categories (family, poetry, occult, notebooks, finished poems, fragments of poems). I've analyzed his book collection for significant annotations and marginalia, cataloguing whatever met a certain threshold.

Gerrit doubted the cleaning service he'd hired could discern between important papers and waste, so he'd always refused to allow them to clean beyond the kitchen. Exposed to a quarter century's worth of accumulated grime and cat dander, I developed breathing problems and for a time became reliant on an inhaler my doctor gave me. And month after month the anxious head count of archival boxes as guests circulated through Gerrit's house until the archive moved to my home in October of 2018. It was, to be frank about it, an ordeal, and one I wouldn't have undertaken if not for my esteem for Gerrit's life and work, one I don't intend to repeat.

Summer cooled to fall, winter came, then spring again.

Gerrit's presence was harder to sense; the books sold – to Adam Davis of Divison Leap, and Sam Burton of Grey Matter, with the remnant four thousand books to Brattle. So the last resonance of Gerrit, the final warmth, departed, the yawning, empty bookcases consolidated in the downstairs library, the walls bare. Mary Catherine Kinniburgh, who somehow managed to swing a trip to Gloucester as she finished the requirements of her doctorate and began a new job at the New York Public Library, took approximately 600 photographs documenting Gerrit's books before they sold.

I can only imagine Gerrit shaking his head in disbelief at the work we've done to ensure his life and writing become a subject of study for future scholars.

When I close the kitchen door for the last time, it takes a leap of imagination and will to conjure Gerrit, his lanky form, short gray hair, baggy sweater, loose jeans, the spotted hand waving when I walk up the drive, saying *Hi Dave, come on in.*

HANGING LOOSE WITH DENISE LEVERTOV

"Against the editorial statement that 'there are
no new forms: free verse is merely another
vehicle,' etc., I pose my belief that the poet, not the
poem is a vehicle."
　　　　　Denise Levertov, An Admonition

　　　Denise Levertov's association with Hanging Loose began
three years before the first issue was ever published. Ron Schreiber,
a teaching assistant at Columbia (he was writing his dissertation
on the poetry of William Carlos Williams) and, Emmett Jarrett, an
undergraduate, teamed up to launch a literary magazine named
"Things," after Williams' "No ideas but in things."

　　　"Things," was a handsome letterpress magazine, but after
three issues it went broke—a brief but not unusual lifespan for a
little magazine. Emmett, who was studying poetry with Denise,
asked her to contribute to the first issue. "An Admonition," her
submission, (later reprinted in her prose collection *The Poet in the*
World) is characteristic of her relationship with Hanging Loose.
Aptly titled, it is a mild, but firm scolding of the editors for, in her
view, too narrowly interpreting Williams' dictum.

　　　Dick Lourie join the editorial board of "Things" for its
final issue. Emmett had met him in 1964 in the workshop Denise
taught at the Manhattan YMHA's Poetry Center and his poems
had appeared in the magazine. Denise considered Emmett and
Dick—and later me, another of her poetry students—to be personal
friends, but our friendships did not prevent her from taking issue
from time to time with the editorial vision or the selection of work
published in Hanging Loose.

　　　When "Things" folded the small press mimeo revolution
was already in full swing. Taking advantage of this cheap, fast,
readily available means of production, Hanging Loose was born in
1966 with Dick, Emmett, Ron, and a new addition, Robert (Bob)
Hershon at its helm. Bob had had poems accepted for "Things."

Dick met with him to explain that, although it was folding, Bob's poems would appear in "Hanging Loose," a new magazine he and the other two editors were launching. Before their meeting ended, Dick persuaded Bob to join this new endeavor. As Bob tells it, "I didn't realize I'd signed-on for a life sentence."

Poems were typed on a stencil, and run off in multiple copies on a mimeo machine. The editors' vision for the magazine, in keeping with the time was that it literally "hang loose," i.e. unbound, loose pages. They held collating parties, inviting local contributors and friends. Everyone circumnavigate a large table from which they picked up the pages from stacks to compile complete copies of the contents. These were then slipped into a white 6 x 9 envelop the cover of which was illustrated by an artist of the editors' acquaintance. A drawing by the prominent New York artist Mimi Gross graced issue #1.

The format was meant to get across a point of view that poetry is for now, not for the Ages. If you liked a poem you could tack it to the wall or give it to a friend. If you didn't like a poem you could toss it in a trash bin or use it as a napkin. The editors were not interested in begging poems from famous writers. They wanted to stress work by new writers and older writers whose work deserved a larger audience.

Denise, who didn't offer any objection to this vision, was invited to be a contributing editor. She continued in that role for the next twenty-plus years. What this entailed was loosely defined. From time to time she would encourage poets whose work she approved of to submit work to Hanging Loose. Some of these poems were published in the magazine, others were rejected. The editors felt no obligation to accept work simply because Denise recommended it. From time to time a poem of her own appeared in the magazine.

On three occasions, the editors asked Denise to edit a special supplement of poems for an issue. For these, colored paper was used or colored ink to distinguish them from the rest, and each included an introduction by Denise. She typically chose poems by her students or other young poets whose work she had encountered and wanted to promote. My association with Hanging Loose began with the first of these Levertov supplements, when Denise gathered poems by the student's in her M.I.T. poetry workshop. It was my first publication.

Although a Brooklyn-based literary magazine since it's early years, soon after its first few issues the editors scattered, Dick to Ithaca, New York, Emmett to Greece for a time, and Ron to Boston, where he joined the English faculty of the University of Massachusetts campus there. Bob was the exception. His home at 231 Wyckoff Street, in the Boerum Hill section of Brooklyn, became--and remains--the official address for Hanging Loose. For a time in the early 1970s, Miguel Ortiz, another student of Denise's and a lifelong New Yorker, joined the editorial staff.

After M.I.T., Denise taught at Brandeis and Tufts universities and lived in Boston eventually settling in Somerville, where Ron also lived. I was introduced to Ron at a dinner party Denise hosted. I subsequently ran into him at poetry readings around the city since I continued to live and to work in the Boston area after completing my degree. Years later, in the late 1970s, when I began teaching at UMass Boston, I was invited to join a men's group of which Ron was a charter member. A friendship resulted.

About this same time, Emmett Jarrett was living in England enrolled in divinity school, soon to be ordained as an Episcopal minister. He hadn't been able to keep up his end of Hanging Loose editorial responsibilities for several years and his absence was sorely felt by the others, all of whom had day jobs that didn't include editing the magazine. Emmett officially resigned and Ron proposed me to take his place, which I did, starting in 1980.

The Supplements

The first supplement Denise edited appeared in *Hanging Loose #12* (1970). Still loose in format, that issue sported a cover illustration by Zevi Blum. The supplement, including Denise's introduction (below) was numbered pages i-xvi, printed on mustard yellow paper. The "regular" pages, numbered 1-52, were printed on cream paper.

Toward a Community of Poets

Poems from M.I.T. Poetry Workshop 1969-1970

Why a group of poems from a class? Well, in this class we tried to get to know one another better than most people usually do in college courses, even in poetry workshops; and to a certain extent we succeeded, at least in that relative degree. We met in each other's apartments (not everyone's, though, as some lived in dorms or very small rooms or awkward locations) and most of us spent a weekend together on Cape Cod. The point of all this, aside from the fact that it was fun, was to help people trust and understand each other so that their *mutual aid*, their criticism and response, could be both franker and more sensitive. My hope was that they would feel themselves, however ephemerally, a *community of poets*, and never as competitive aspirants for approval. It is in the belief that there were some radiant moments, at least, when that community did exist, and that even when it did not it was hovering on the edge of being, that I have gathered this group of poems, one from each. The choice had, for the usual reasons of space, to be among short poems, so that this selection does not accurately 'represent' most people's work so far, especially those who undertook much longer poems. For almost all, this is their first publication, and because of the friendships and good feeling that came into being during the year, it seems appropriate that this should be something shared. As for me, I can't believe I'll ever work with a bunch of people dearer and more fascinating to me.

Denise Levertov

The workshop was an M.I.T. course in name only, reflecting the fact that Denise had unconventional ideas about teaching, some

239

of which she articulated in her essay "The Untaught Teacher." (*The Poet in the World*) Its title points to the fact that Denise herself was never formally schooled. (She was homeschooled by her mother, with supplemental lessons from BBC radio.)

About half the students enrolled in the workshop *were* M.I.T. students, but the rest came from Harvard, Radcliffe, Simons College, and Northeastern University, plus one carpenter, one oceanographer, and one UC Berkeley student (Aaron Shurin) who followed her east six months after she had taught a poetry class on that campus. (My essay "Wordsmiths in the Idea Factory" in *Denise Levertov in Company*, Donna Krolik Hollenberg, Ed., University of South Carolina Press, 2017, gives a detailed description of this workshop). Many of this workshop's alumni have continued to write and publish poems, often with encouragement from Denise, and not a few have produced multiple collections of their work: Arthur Sze, Judy Katz-Levine, Aaron Shurin, Richard Edelman, Margo Taft Stever, and me.

Two more Levertov edited Hanging Loose supplements appeared over the next dozen years.

Hanging Loose # 21, 1973
(2 color, unbound. Supplement: 20 out of 72 pages total)
SPECIAL SUPPLEMENT
Edited by Denise Levertov
Introduction

This collection of poems by young poets whose work I find moving to me as a reader and stimulating to me as a writer includes no women writers, for the simple practical reason that I am currently editing a group of poems by women for *Trellis* (c/o Irene McKinney, 136 James Street, Morgantown, West Virginia 26505) and in both cases I have only about 20 pages to work (or play) with. There are a number of other people I would like to have included here. I am resisting the temptation to name them, lest I forget an essential name. However, those I have included represent something of the variety and energy that exists among unknown writers in their early to mid-twenties. A few of those I would have included if I'd had more space or if I'd written to ask for poems instead of depending on what I had in my desk drawer—burning and shining in there, wanting out! —are over 30, but I would in any case have focused on the young because I find in their work a sense of process from which I personally draw more nourishment than from all but a few of my contemporaries, though there are many of those that I *admire*. Curiously, I find more of this same sense of process in the generation of Williams, Stevens, Pound, than in the poets of my own generation. The old masters of the century and the best of the still very young, far though they may be from mastery, share, for me, some peculiar force.

Denise Levertov

This supplement of ten poets included three who had appeared in the previous, M.I.T. class, supplement: Richard Edelman, Aaron Shurin, and me.

Hanging Loose #43, 1982-83
(3 color matt cover, 88 pages perfect bound. The supplement comprises 30 pages printed in blue ink, the rest printed in black.)
SUPPLEMENT:POEMS FROM DENISE LEVERTOV'S MAILBOX
Introduction

My aesthetic relationship with the editors of "Hanging Loose" as editors (they are also my cherished friends) has always in some degree been that of a friendly adversary. I am thinking back to the direct precursor of "Hanging Loose," the magazine called "Things," which Emmett Jarrett (one of the original editors of "Hanging Loose") and Ron Schreiber started in 1963. Only three issues of "Things" appeared. And the first one included a sort of letter from me, 'An Admonition' (afterward reprinted in *The Poet in the World*) in which I hailed the naming of a magazine

241

after Williams' 'No ideas but in things' but objected to the narrow definitions the editors' prospectus proposed. When "Things" died and was immediately reborn as "Hanging Loose" (acquiring, over time, some additional editors and eventually losing some of the earlier ones). I was listed as contributing editor, a role I've filled both in the accepted manner, i.e., by recommending the magazine to various students, friends and acquaintances as one to which they should submit work, and sometimes telling the editors about some poet I specially recommended; and also--thanks to their editorial courtesy--by occasionally taking the opportunity to edit a special supplement. One of these, in the early 70's, was of the work of students I had been teaching; another featured some then recent new discoveries or enthusiasms of mine. In both cases the supplements probably included poems the actual editorial board of "Hanging Loose" would have rejected, just as each issue of the magazine has included poems I would have rejected. That's not surprising, since boards always arrive at choices by a difficult consensus process, and consensus is not necessarily wholehearted unanimity. But beyond that normal degree of individual difference of taste, I think there's probably a greater difference between my taste and that of "Hanging Loose's" board as a group than between any members of that board. And yet I care about, and respect, the magazine. I am vicariously proud of its already long life (as little magazines go, it will soon be positively elderly!) and I am happy that this aesthetic difference has not alienated us from one another. What is, or are, the divergent values, then--and what do we share?

I think we share a contempt for mere careerism, and for the 'clone poetry,' (to use Sam Hamill's phrase) of M.F.A. Programs which so often foster both cloning and careerist ambitions; we share a respect for honesty, for a sense of necessity--for poems that convince one that they had to be written, that the poet didn't feel that he or she had a choice in the matter. We share a delight in discovering poems of social engagement that actually are poems; and a concern for finding and celebrating--by publication--the young, the unknown, and the undeservedly neglected of any age.

We share an instinctive distrust of the utilization of poetry as a fancy-dress costume for pompous philosophizing--and thus, any poetry that seems to smell of the library carrel rather than of the air of streets or fields, kitchens or living rooms, might be read by any of us with caution, even with some prejudice against it (though the library can in fact be a place as replete with vivid experience as any other, it is well to remember--but the poem's smell must be of the living moments known there, and not of library glue...). We share a basic political outlook. And we share a love of the work and principles of William Carlos Williams, who of all American major poets has been for each of us the one we've looked to most as mentor and example. That's a lot.

But where I differ from them has to do with degrees and kinds of music and rhetoric, I think. The poems they've published which I would have rejected are, to my ear, 'flat.' Now, Dick Lourie's own poetry, which I admire and love, could often be described as 'flat': he doesn't "go in" for melopoeia. But his work has so definite and authentic a personal voice, and presents such a unique blending of comedy and strong seriousness, that 'flatness' becomes, in it, simply an ingredient, used to such effect that it no longer is mere flatness; whereas I've seen many poems in "Hanging Loose" over the years, (as in too many other magazines) that seem to simply disregard musicality--sometimes from inability to produce it, I suspect, but perhaps, in other cases, as a result of confusing musicality with the sound and fury of an outworn 'academic', or 'mandarin' mode. Which brings me to my basis of choice for this supplement: I have not simply tried to look for musically satisfying poems; rather my hunch was that I would find, by random selection from among those I had recently received in the mail, many which would not, I believed, betray those values this 'contributing editor' shares with the real editors, yet which would carry in various ways, some other elements: music, magic, mystery of some kind, something that would draw me to them in the first instance and make me feel I would want to read them again years hence.

243

I believe that hunch was right. Call this group of poems 'Levertov's choice', if you will: certainly it is personal, subjective even. But is it not of some interest to observe that I did not have to hunt up the poems, but that almost all of them simply floated my way like dandelion clocks? As I did, I should in fairness add, plenty of other poems I did not like, for I am not claiming that no selection process took place. But it took place from among poems I happened to encounter this past winter. The qualities I was hoping for were there to be found. Here, then, this cluster:

"Levertov's Choice" included poems by Sam Hamill, Abby Niebauer, Bonnie Bishop, Charles Grace Anastas, Stephen Strempek, Susan Eisenberg, Maria Damon, Graham Leggat, David Walton Wright, Paula Denham, Susan Glickman, Jacob Leed, Jimmy Santiago Baca, Steven Blevins, and Rick Stansberger.

The parting of ways that Denise attributed to aesthetic differences as indicated by her introduction to the 1982 supplement came to a head five years later when Dick Lourie received the following letter from her on Stanford University stationery but addressed to all four editors: (Denise taught poetry each spring semester at Stanford for many years.)

Feb. 11, 1987
Dear Dick, Bob, Ron, & Mark,

Don't take this as hostility to Hanging Loose—it's truly not—but I do want to have my name off the masthead. There are 2 reasons: 1. There are other magazines I like as well, & often better, than H.L., & I feel placed in a false position by my association with this one magazine, as if it represented my preferences in contemporary poetry. While there are often items in it that I do like, it does not embody my enthusiasms & biases. You and I know the reasons for my association with it—long ago, & in continuing friendships. But readers do not Thus a false message is conveyed.

2. I am in a stage of life where I am trying to divest myself of more & more encumbrances—sharply reducing the amount of mail I answer, even if I lose some friends in the process; cutting

down many social engagements even if they are tempting; doing
less traveling (only the work-travel I have to do to pay the bills,
while foregoing whatever pleasure-travel does not seem likely
to contribute to my creative life); & so forth. Now, although my
name on H.L. doesn't involve me in any labor, it is time: even the
occasional letter you send on is usually not something I personally
deal with. Yet you have to take my word for it that it has been a
symbolic significance for me.

I appreciate the honor of your wanting me to change
my mind. But I will appreciate even more the understanding of
friendship which will now let me take this small symbolic step
of divesting myself of one of the multitude of small threads &
hindrances from which I have a deep need to free myself.

Love & best wishes,

Denise

P.S. If you want to just remove it quietly, without drawing attention
to the fact, it wd. Probably be best. But if you prefer, you can put
in a notice which wd. prevent readers from thinking that some
quarrel is behind the move, e.g. some very summary of point 2
above—not mentioning point 1 in case it might harm the magazine
in the minds of some people.

Of course, we acquiesced to Denise's request and removed
her name from the masthead. But this termination of our twenty-
plus year association didn't come as a surprise, not that any of
the editors welcomed it. Then in November of 1990, Denise sent
a testy note via Dick again, but addressed to Bob. It's "cease and
desist" tone complained about our continued use of a blurb she
had written long ago to promote Emmett Jarrett's poetry collection
God's Body.

Although published in 1975, one of the first Hanging Loose
titles, Emmett's book, like every other, past and present, was still
in print regardless of the fact it hadn't sold a copy in years. Like all
other titles it was listed in the Hanging Loose catalog and, like the
others, with its original blurb. Denise's pique struck us as strange

given that she had been receiving copies of the catalog for more than a decade without ever objecting to the reprinting of her blurb.

That was the last communique the Hanging Loose editors received from Denise. I've wondered if she wasn't already feeling the effects of the lymphoma that took her life several years later.

"Levertov's Mailbox" prompted speculative discussions among us editors as to Denise's real reasons for terminating the relationship. There was a sense of "she doth protest too much" in the very lengthy commentary, "Notes on Poems and Poets," she included in the final supplement. Quite unlike the brief biographical information–name, college, major–that accompanied the MIT supplement, and the very brief group identification in her introduction to the second supplement: "poets in their early to mid-twenties" with a common "sense of process," her "Notes" about the individual poets in the final supplement (not included here) ran to three pages, the same length as her introduction to her selection.

"Levertov's Mailbox" perplexed us and her subsequent communique rekindled in us questions about her motivation. Her rationales never rang entirely true, in part because she never identified specific poets or poems published in the magazine as illustrations of the aesthetic differences she alluded to. The accusation of an editorial bias in favor of "flatness" over musicality in poems was something we found baffling. As to the poems she herself selected, we weren't persuaded of significant differences from the poems we had chosen. (Two of the poets in Denise selected have appeared multiple times in issues of Hanging Loose, chosen by us editors: Rick Stansberger (twice) and David Walton Wright (five times, over a span of forty years).

Was it our aesthetic closeness to 2nd and 3rd generation New York School poets she objected to? But that never meant we excluded poems inspired by the example and principles of William Carlos Williams. Did she detect in us a preference for poems in the mode of Robert Creeley in contrast to her other cherished poet friend Galway Kinnell? Didn't the two exhibit different kinds of rhetoric and degrees of musicality both of which she, once at least, embraced? Did Paul Violi's sly, sometimes raucously humorous poems that we often published offend her sense of the seriousness of the Poet's vocation? Or was she simply tone deaf to poems that referenced popular American culture as when she once inquired about a mention of basketball in one: "Is that the game where they throw a something through a hoop?"

And we speculated that the changed nature of some of our friendships combined with new influences on our individual poetic tastes beyond those she had introduced us to so many years before were also contributing factors. Whatever it was that offended her sensibilities, none of us felt inclined to debate her point by point.

Legacy

Since its inception, 110 issues of Hanging Loose magazine have appeared and more than 250 book titles are in print, and we keep on keeping on. One thing that hasn't changed in 53 years is the process by which we editors choose poems to include in any issue. It is a legacy of our relationship with Denise. Dick, Emmett, Miguel Ortiz, and me, as one-time students of hers learned directly from her the value of poetry's orality; i.e., the importance of taking in a poem by way of the ear (wasn't that Olson's phrase?). Although never her students, the merits of this approach were obvious to Bob and Ron.

The preponderance of poems published in Hanging Loose magazine come across the transom in Brooklyn. After the obvious duds are rejected, the rest are slipped into a large manila envelope with routing slips attached for the recording of votes and put in the mail to be circulated among the editors. (Yes, we're old fashion. We don't use an electronic submission manager and we read every poem we receive.)

Roughly every three months we three editors (Ron having passed away in 2004) gather for a weekend, these days mostly in Brooklyn. We sit around a table piled high with the manuscripts that have survived the initial reading process and, taking turns, we read aloud each poem that has received a positive vote.

After we have *heard* the poem read aloud, we discuss and vote anew whether to include it in the next issue or not, discounting whether the route slip shows it received Yes votes, indicating it made a strong positive impression on first reading, or whether it received a single Maybe vote, indicating perceived merits and worthy of further consideration. Regardless how a poem strikes us when read on the page, the deciding factor is how well it works when taken in by way of the ear. Were Denise Levertov still alive, I'm confident this is one Hanging Loose editorial practice she would approve of.

The Editors Editing
>
> By Robert Hershon

Nomi our neighbor
Asks Donna what are those
Guys doing out back
Sitting around the table
Table full of papers
And one guy goes blah blah blah blah
And the others all shake their heads
And go ahum ahum ahum

Then the oaks leaves fall
Then the white garden furniture
Covered with gray city snow
Bluejay walks across the table
And down somebody's leg
Blah blah blah blah

SAM CORNISH: PLAYING THE CHANGES

"He said to play on the changes until he left them, and then just follow him. At first I thought he meant he would play on the written changes for a little while, but then I realized he would be creating a new set of changes almost right away..."

> *Charlie Haden on playing with Ornette Coleman (from Ethan Iverson, "Interview with Charlie Haden," March 2008)*

Folks Like Me by Sam Cornish, more than any other book, introduced me to the pleasures of a well-wrought and resonant sequence of poems. Not a collection, bundle, or sheaf. But a constellated sequence, a set, a book. Also, not a concept album, anti-epic, or epic; though containing history. Not a polyvocal narrative, sonnet cycle, or docupoem; though containing plenty of information and proper nouns (and a glossary). No, *Folks Like Me* is something else.

Folks Like Me foregrounds Black American experiences and culture within the larger context of American culture and history. Aptly, in class and conversation, Cornish often invoked Ralph Ellison's formulation: "Despite his racial difference and social status, something indisputably American about Negroes not only raised doubts about the white man's value system, but aroused the troubling suspicion that whatever else the true American is, he is also somehow black." Cornish's poems include the 20th century and the past, women and men, the South and the North, working class and middle class, honky-tonks and churches, work of the hands and of the mind. The arrangement is thoughtful, evocative—sometimes playful, never fussy, ever *on point*. In other words, Cornish plays the changes. Cornish navigates thematic variations, like an improvising musician navigating chord changes within a harmonic environment, introducing subtle, satisfying, and substantial modulations. And just when readers think they've sussed out the possibilities, Cornish weaves in a new thematic set. And the reader follows.

The book begins with a prose poem that, like the head of a jazz tune, introduces themes that Cornish then plays with in subsequent poems—improvisation with substitutions. Here, as throughout the book, themes recur and entwine. Each permutation is comprised of recognizable elements from the head but the particular use and the substitutions make it new. Cornish's blues prosody—evident in every poem—is informed by playing the changes—improvising on themes-as-chords—within *Folks Like Me* and within each of his books. The poems are blues; the books are bop.

That's the form—or a metaphor for the form—but the matters matter more.

Folks Like Me begins with women, as do three of Cornish's other books, *Sam's World, 1935: A Memoir, and An Apron Full of Beans. Folks Like Me* opens with family women and their work: "my mother did day work, my grandmother was a domestic." And here as elsewhere he is interested in the intersectionality of gender, race, and class: "These women speak of the domestic maid who had spent her life with the (white) family (who she never admired) and some of these households thought the maid—or at least they said—was family." He plays the changes on the complexities and power dynamics of whites and blacks, men and women, rich and poor intertwined. Later in the poem, he is thinking about "white women who cannot understand the sit-ins or Jesse Jackson," and he dedicates the book to "Southern women...black women, white women." In starting here, as in so many of his books, he is explicitly mindful from the very first words that "These women tell another story," a story the reader is unlikely to know and especially unlikely to know intimately and in its many permutations. Cornish is present to hear the story told, and he does more than catch the gist: he distills the song.

The next four poems play the changes of that song. Poems about Harriet Tubman, Sojourner Truth, a woman who refuses to give up her seat to a white man in 1932, and a girl named Mary develop the theme of women's burdens, strength, and courage. These poems sing the blues and pay respect. Tubman is "General Moses"; Sojourner ("like Harriet") wants to "pull...my people through the forest" and "forge those mighty rivers." "Sojourner" revisits the interactions of black women and white women found in the head poem: "what do white/women/see when they think/of me   speak those words I spoke[?]" The woman who refuses to give up her seat also links back to the first poem ("Perfect Day") when she introduces herself as "a working woman/an all/day woman." The fifth poem, "Horseface," drops the theme of women's work but introduces another burden, a permutation of the black/white question: "oh she was so/black her father/passed out/(he wanted to lighten/the race..."

The sixth poem of the collection, "Honky Tonk," provides a hinge: opening onto the explicit presence of the blues as subject and swinging back to another variation on the theme *what-women-do-to-provide*: "my mother a rough neck/busting heads/for a pair of shoes/these people the music/in my horn".

And so the book proceeds with Cornish playing the changes and deepening the blues, creating multiple and overlapping echoes and mutations. The seventh poem, "America As a Cabin," ends with the lines "the promised land/of a common man   something/new something white," lines which evoke, twist, and deepen the painful and ineluctable encounter with internalized racism found at the end of "Horseface": Mary "sought/love from people going North/as her father did/somewhere lighter/someplace better." Playing the changes is more than style; it's a way to cut to the heart of the intersection of race and personal, familial, regional, and national history.

Cornish's playing cuts. Cornish "is a sharpener and a sander and a honer," writes Amiri Baraka; "This is a poetry of the ice pick..." writes James Tate. Cornish's language is a sharpened pick to get to the heart. The pick picks the tune and cuts the track—ever-changing but familiar every time.

In *Folks Like Me*, work—linked to women's domestic work in the first poem—becomes the agricultural work of men in "Workers of the Soil" which becomes the proud work of men *and women* at the end of "Elegy". There's a seed of protest in the poem "Workers of the Soil" (hands are "like marching feet") that is transubstantiated into dignified pride by Booker T. Washington's ethos in "If the Negro Cannot See Work As Honorable" and "Elegy" before blossoming into the defiance of three poems informed by African-American engagement with Communism: "Not Long for That Day," "Coke Bottle Glasses," and "Annals of the Poor." The shift across these poems is also a shift among autobiographical, folkloric, and historical sources. And to make the book really sing, woven between and within these poems about work are lines and poems about the¬ work disrupting seductions of jazz, booze, and sex and the salve of pious religious devotion. Then, launching out of these initial Communism-informed poems are subsequent poems about "The Lincoln Brigade," Paul Robeson (twice), the film *My Son John*, Sacco and Vanzetti, J. Edgar Hoover, Howard Fast, Ben Davis, and Black Bolsheviks.

And so on.

Tracing the changes played on other themes-as-chords one finds violence, marches, trains, uncles, Uncle Remus and a friend named John. And true to the title, one finds a panoply of poets and writers—more folks like Sam: Claude McKay, Thoreau, Dickens, Hawthorne, Thoreau (again), Owen Dodson, Joel Chandler

Harris, Ellison, Wright's Bigger Thomas , Paul Lawrence Dunbar, Langston Hughes, Sterling Brown, Joel Chandler Harris (again), Phyllis Wheatley, Claude McKay (again), Howard Fast (twice), Joel Chandler Harris (a third time), Hemingway, Faulkner, Himes, Rand's *Fountainhead*, Wright's Bigger Thomas (again), Larry Neal, Dunbar (again), Wheatley (again), Hughes (again), James Baldwin, and Robert Hayden.

Cornish plays the changes, and each new variation is haunted by what came before and projects into what is to come. Each of Cornish's books lends itself to this sort of reading, which is one of the great pleasures of returning to them again and again. Nuance becomes novelty.

And there's always more than one way to play the changes.

Cornish was my teacher and mentor at Emerson College. On the first day of my second course with him, he came upon my name while taking roll; he paused then said, "James Cook...smokes good weed." Although I didn't and I don't, Cornish was playing the changes. I'm not exactly sure what he was up to, but I think it goes something like this: my name reminded him of a relative, maybe an uncle, who liked the finer things, whereas I was inhibited and a great target for teasing. I was repressed and a mess. And Cornish knew something about me and pleasure that I didn't yet know— though he got the details a bit wrong. In any case, I think he saw my need before I did, so he played with it, made a little song out of it as he read the roll on that first day of class. He was funny that way.

A year or so later, during office hours, he said something similar. He asked about my shelves of books, wondered where I put the hard covers. At the time I had no shelves. All of my books—about a dozen—were in a box under my bed, but he knew something about the train that was coming for me. He knew before I did about

253

the room I'm sitting in now, books filling the shelves along every surface, stacks of books (each for a different project) on nearly every surface.

These two moments come together like poems in one of his books, speaking to each other across variations of cadence, tone, diction, audience, and occasion. Cornish was funny that way, playing the changes and cutting—pick sharp—to the quick.

POEMS FOR WILLIAM CORBETT

Energy

For Bill Corbett

He insisted on getting to Gerrit's memorial
At Gloucester's Hammond Castle by the sea.

Fanny walked him up the aisle.
He spoke, I couldn't hear what he said.
His face was unrecognizable.

Our Man in Boston, as Creeley called him.
You felt the energy in his red round face.

He conducted, eyes closed,
to nail the rhythms while the poets read.
He was the one who had brought them there.

There's so much to think about
I guess I'll go home.
The last time he was at my house

He said,
As he was leaving, with a mutinous smile,
'Thanks for the gossip.'

He treated poetry with respect.

We read at Steve Lacy's memorial

At St. Mark's, thanks to Creeley.
I saw Bill standing in the wings and,
Intimidated by him then, the only thing
I could think of to say was,
'Where's the bathroom?'
If I remember right, 'Over there'
Is what he answered, and he patted me on the head.

He was a little shy, too, and a little sweet.
But he loved to turn up the heat.

One and Eight

I was wading in the ocean waters
In Ship Bottom, New Jersey
When I heard it in the waves of the tide
Bill Corbett had passed away

It was 8.10.18
the numbers
stung with the sinking feeling of loss
eight and ten   eighteen
one and eight
nine and nine take us back

A solitary figure and infinity
Crazy eights and the missing one
Carry the one through the maze of eights
The Hebrew word chai
Meaning life
Has a numerical value of eighteen.

Joseph Heller originally titled
Catch-22 Catch-18 for the
Hebrew significance of the number.

Ulysses has eighteen chapters
There are also eighteen chapters in the Bhagavad Gita
Which is part of the Mahabharata which has
eighteen books.

The Tarot Card 18
the moon dripping tears

The Virgin Mary appearing holy

To Bernadette a total of eighteen times

Eighteen years ago, Bill
Toasting John Wieners
At 9 Columbus Square
Champagne and caviar,
Raising glasses to Pressed Wafer
The Body of Christ
The perfect circle
Seamus Heaney sneaking in
leaving a bottle of whiskey
on the table
John smiling uncomfortably in his winter coat
Dreaming of eighteen sailors to take him away
On Fair Winds
and
Following seas.
Bill removed his glasses
And looked skyward

Shocked when we last met
In the Hammond castle
On 2.24.18 (Eight One Eight)
To celebrate the pure light passing
Of Gerrit Lansing
Bill's body broken
His whisper waned as
We hugged and
he slipped the last
Pressed Wafer
into my hand.

Poems for Bill Corbett by Michael Franco

*Note: This is a run of peoms all of which circulate
or address directly the 30+ years of friendship
with Bill Corbett*

from How to Live: Zoland Books 1998
  TUESDAY MAY 3rd 1988, 6:12PM
I write this day,
that you are gone
& still I write
*"sentence after sentence I make
in your image"*
This sentence you are
now finished with
I continue
within
the learning I lack
or the references that I can   not remember
move   no more
than a shadow on a sidewalk
           changing as I pass   beneath the tall street light

out   out
each brief passing

remains

A post card brought us here
  called this
dance-we-are
each step
Fate's agents
too often so simple

-a fluttering of paper
the greeks would have heard wings
& wondered what
disguised god or Oracle
had blest them
  with a sign
these words might have been
a narrow passage in the movement
always quickening
Aware
we watch
Unaware we are no more
than a shadow
of our own
dancing
turn on turn
the post card fluttering
fluttering
to the floor
What would be
let loose into
an acute choreography
within which we turn
proceeding to now

Clumsy
as usual
I did not see
  the outstretched
hand the foot-fall

                              turn

& fall
reaching

Silence

stretching out
between desk and floor
juggling the air
to retrieve
this accumulation
of correspondences
as they pass

*[I sent this to Bill as an announcement that I had returned from Portugal with more
than a bottle of port...... two years later he conducted my marriage to Isabel .....
standing in the articulated silence of a falling snow outside the windows of our living
room in Arlington Ma. Beverly and Molly Torra as Maids of Honor, Joe Torra, Best
Man ... on January 7th 1994.]*

---

there   is
a   bell
        that   once struck
will not stop ringing

    one of the old stories
that rimes   in us   words
that will not translate
        each time   we leave   or are left
Silence   Distance   Death
    dark Sisters of each day
go with us   and this is not sadness
nor unnatural

river that is sound words that are a river
speak to us ask us
is a bell
silent once struck

it is not   but lingers out of sight of the ear
        harmony   hears
from such distance
        aroused   cat-like expectation
        at the periphery of what we can know
is the order of   these things
each step returns to us
carries us
on its own melody
we hear only echoe's vast harmony
surrounding
do not turn back but carry
what resonance   you can
this that is remembered
        you are
and will   with each hour each day
        the years that   will pass   as hours not ours

        remain

[Sunday morning, May 10th 1992 @ Coimbra

For Those Gathered & for my Wife
    on our 15th [January 11th12:30pm green line/ in route to Beverly

and it is that particular
Light of the Stars
which divides the surrounding

darks into separate
contingencies as the
days– the years–

now   gather

around us just enough

to call

our notice

itself
a dance of
delights whose
turns or terms

we name
Joe we name Molly
Katha Tom
Ben Judy

Ed   Jenny
Chris Patricia

Beverly and Bill

new friends found while for others
small candles   left out
on a window
to echo this
sky I am thinking of
the Love
we all bridle
at   call

collect with a
glance a touch
another

fine meal

  another

Day
   offered up

to such

_____

{poem for LIFT: Corbett Issue}

_for william corbett
[from ms of 12 17 02:
/12 19 02; pm] &8or so pm same day

behind every painter
there   is
a landscape
whose   reach is horizon
who launches color into late sky
who holds gull high upon invisibility
across which sun rise sun set spills illuminated
hills or lilac twinning vines of clematis soft
dust of peony long and green hedge rows of asparagus tips
singular trees seeming alone tall and thick barked
home of all birds and stiff with bugs in twilight gatherings
across which
in looking all
or at least every
thing is
drawn every glance a quick sketch
every walk gathering
   leaves

twin-faced float to ground
us looking
as we do
across breadth of
yesterday and what ever
is to come

---

dec 4th 2003, Barrett/ Corbett reading

So the days begin to accumulate
                    a Nor'easter   life makes
                    running up the coast of a year
until so many names collect
against the back door that
you can't get it open anymore and I would
call out but how would I choose amongst the ghosts
of the living from all of the thoughts that I have
of their fact or fiction

Moments gust and slip beyond reach
An evening comes to an end
A name arrives in the course of a line like a quick kiss in greeting,
some linger a moment longer than   proper and a relationship
develops out of time place or circumstance
intimate, alone,   close
 call it
influence

but

give me the thoughts
if you will let them
spill out across the horizon of anything I might know and
the good ones gust and take me away for one of those moments

like tonight
where these two friends sit awkward
words disarranged and read to us to themselves
without measure
this is what Love is what defines friendship
this is the only reason
for following these lines as they
cross my page.

————————————————————

____for Bill...10th August 2018 ....126pm @ Oxford Street

   the porcelain preciousness
of so many fine things rests only
in the illusion of a firm hug an offered hand a meal
gone so gone in laughter and stories
that you almost forget to eat–
 a post card whose ancient message flutters to the floor
from the opening of a book

....fugitive time and grace contained that almost   seems to sail

on the empty air calling

to be retrieved

Dear Bill

Another Boston April
And still no spring.
Raw March did nothing
But grate. Older
I grow more I hate
These no-springs
And everything
They bring—cold,
Rain, wind, spitting
snow. My bones
No longer
Tolerate. No
Matter how many
Layers under my
Old black leather—
Same one after all
These years, when
Do you let a jacket go?
Three weeks from
Now Julia graduates—
Julia, who you wrote
A letter for college
Admissions, whose
Arrival in America
Attended by you
And Beverly and Arden.
Jonas wrote that years
Pass like water.
And Celeste has
Killed it in her
Freshman year,
Home soon for
The summer, if

It ever comes.
Last time we talked
Was over an hour—
Lucia Berlin
My 6 American Authors
Course—and yes
The students loved her
The way we do.
What's the most
People ever for dinner
At 9 Columbus?
How many glasses
Of wine for me there,
And arguments, and
Foolish things I regret
Saying? You taught
Me to be true
To my vulgarities.
My teacher.
I blame you
For everything. When
You first read
Gas Station you
Congratulated me
On writing the book
That you were still
Unable to write.
What praise for
A Dago from the
Medford street corner.
You hurt me.
I hurt you.
Forgive Us.
We knew, or knew
Not what we do.

Remember the day
We walked Kerouac's Lowell
My feet blistered
My engineer boots?
Too cool, still am,
For good walking shoes.
Charlie's lunch!
Bob's big subs!
Clayton Eshleman!
Drinks with Eddie B!
No free drinks at
The Wine Cellar.
Too many readings
Like "a bucket of
Dirty dishwater".
Who needs New Critics?
And all that bad
Boston poetry?
"You have some
Good tones, sounds
And rhythms" you
Told me first
time you heard
me read. Word
of Mouth, 1989.
Did you give Eddie
Your socks or he you?
No matter. I
Remember too much
Wine and Michael's whole
Salmon with a Champagne
Cream. My father
Gave me two pieces
Of good advice:
Mix pork with your

Meatballs and never
Wear white socks
When you dress up.
I still hate him.
I got my vision
For Tony Luongo
Riding shotgun with you
That old Packard
In Vermont. What
A ride. Memory
Slides in slippery
Tracks. Can't go
Back except in
The imagination.
I think of Williams
Spring and All.
He knew.
But that day
In the Packard
There was someone
To drive the car.
And somewhere
Along a country road
I saw the entire novel
Right before my eyes.
First day back home
Began banging out
Those pages, not
Letting up until
That last period-less word.
That's why it was
Your book. Who
Gave me permission
To do what I
Could do. What

I was meant to do.
Standardization
Be fucking damned.
I never told you
One day, Molly
And I were in
The South End—
I did not know you
Well enough yet
We saw you and
Your family walking
Down Columbus Ave.
I told her that's Bill
Corbett the poet—
At one point you
Stepped ahead, turned
And made crazy gestures
At Bev and the girls in fun.
Looking out the window
At a dirty gray sky
My mind will not settle,
Stomach growling,
Head pounding for
Some kind of meaning
In all the disorder. Gerrit
Gone. Jonas gone.
Wieners gone.
Li Po and Tu Fu gone.
Basil gone.
My mother too.
The weather
Ruthless and unrelenting.
Someone raise a flag
To the Goddess of
Compassion and Mercy

And I will get down
On my knees, sing
Praises to the past
And the future so
Cold and stony.
Only in the dark night
Tossing and turning,
Mind racing, is the
Emptiness so clear
And believable.
You and Ed and
Me and Behrle
Backseat balling
That jack to NYC—
Smoking weed
On the Merit—
And dinner at Monty's
Four of us drinking
Late into the frigid night—
Ed dared Jim to jump
Into the Gowanus!
Today I walked
Around Walden Pond
Stood at the exact
Spot where the
Photo of you and John
And Lewis and Lee.
Julia told me
After I die
She will tattoo
One of my poems
On her back
"But preferably
Not that long one
You just wrote."

Patrick Pritchett

This Be the Verse You Grave for Me, Or Ride Lonesome

i.m. Bill Corbett, 1942-2018

In the history of secure response there is
always a slight tremble. A warble. An undoing.
A divine and divinatory sunset to which
we cannot quite adjust it goes us south so swiftly
that any fathom of touch fails of return.

In the history of secure response
we are always too much with ourselves he said.
There were dumplings and porridge
and ice cold beers but no Big Papi.
No maps to find a route to Wrack Tavern or Charlie's.

Something golden falls, a softness – a form of air
that unravels every care. We live it says
inside the cults of the famous and the dead
and can never be delivered of them
only more deeply mired and pledged.

The microtonal intervals of longing
signal the fate of misbelonging. We all have
death inside us, growing there, day by day.
Some determine to become elated. Some
embrace magnetic fields. Waves and radiation.

But the ghost is always the scene of writing.
OK, computer, no anthems for the other world
just a small hummable tune: not Mozart nor Trane nor Bey
but it will have to do. Pour your misery down.
There are some things a man can't ride around.

CONTRIBUTORS

Alexei Alexandrov was born in 1968 in the coincidentally homophonous city of Alexandrov in the Vladimir Region of Russia. He graduated from Saratov State University and continues to live Saratov, where he serves as poetry editor of Volga magazine. He is the author of three books of poems: *Ne pokidaya svoikh multfilmov* ("Without leaving his cartoons," NYC, 2013), *Eto byli torpedy dobra* ("Those Were Torpedoes of the Good," Saratov, 2018), and *Molchashchie sledy* ("Silent Tracks," NYC, 2019).

Mikhail Ayzenberg, born in Moscow in 1948, is the author of ten collections of poetry and of several volumes of highly influential critical essays. Prior to 1989, he worked as an architectural restorer. He was a member of the Almanac Poetry Group in the late 1980s and early 1990s. Since then he has lived chiefly as a writer and editor. He also taught at the Russian State University for the Humanities. He has been well translated into foreign languages and holds several major literary awards, including the Andrei Bely Prize (2008) and the Moscow Reckoning Prize (2016).

Raquel Balboni's poems have appeared or are forthcoming in *Art & Letters, The Boston Compass, The Brooklyn Rail, The Charles River Journal, Gianthology* and in the anthology *Boston* (Dostoevsky Wannabe). They live in Cambridge, Massachusetts.

Polina Barskova was born in Leningrad in 1976. Her latest, tenth poetic volume in Russian, *Solnechnoe utro na ploshchadi* ("A Sunny Morning in the Square"), has recently come out in Saint Petersburg. Her three poetry collections translated into English are *This Lamentable City* (Tupelo Press, 2010); *The Zoo in Winter: Selected Poems* (Melville House, 2011); and *Relocations* (Zephyr Press, 2015). She received the 2015 Andrey Bely Prize for her prose volume, Living Pictures, later adapted into a play and staged in Moscow's Theatre of Nations. A professor of Russian literature at Hampshire College, Barskova researched and edited *Written in the*

Dark: Five Poets in the Siege of Leningrad (Ugly Duckling Presse, 2016).

David Blair is the author of five books, *Ascension Days, Friends with Dogs, Arsonville, Walk Around: Essays on Poetry and Place*, and the forthcoming collection, *Barbarian Seasons*. www.davidblairpoetry.com

Olga Bragina (b. 1982) is a poet, author, and translator. A resident of Kyiv, Ukraine, she is bilingual and has published poetry in both Russian and Ukrainian. She graduated from the Translation Department of Kyiv National Linguistic University. Bragina's three poetry collections are *Applikatsii* ("Applications," 2011), *Neymdropping* ("Namedropping," 2012), and *Fonovyi svet* ("Background Light," 2018). Her work has also appeared in a wide range of literary journals and anthologies internationally. Her Russian translation of John High's collection Vanishing Acts came out in Kyiv in 2018.

Olga Chugai (1944-2015) was outstanding poet and an influential figure in Russian poetry. An early adopter of free verse among poets of the Soviet period, she also excelled at traditional and hybrid poetic forms. Her collections include *Sudba gliny* ("The Life of Clay," 1982) and her selected poems, *Svetlye storony t'my* ("The Bright Sides of Darkness," 1995). She edited an important two-volume anthology of Russian poets of her generation, *Grazhdane nochi* ("Citizens of Night," 1990-2). Chugai founded and was the leader of the First Book Laboratory at the USSR Writer's Union in 1977-90, a body that facilitated the publication of first books by many subsequently acclaimed new poets. A volume of her collected works is in preparation. Philip Nikolayev's translations are published with the approval of the Olga Chugai estate.

Amanda Cook lives in Gloucester with her husband, James, and children Abigail and Samuel. She sees writing as an integral part of life. She knits, spins yarn, plays fiddle, feeds people and dances when she pleases. She teaches and works at the Gloucester

Writers Center. Her book, *Ironstone Whirlygig*, was published by Bootstrap Press in 2017.

James Cook signifies and represents in Gloucester, Massachusetts. He fathers-forth but presents change. He husbands. He has worked in high school education for more than twenty years. He has been the co-editor of the literary magazine *Polis*, and his work has appeared in *Wards of the Wards, Let the Bucket Down, Jacket2, Process, Gaff,* and *Underutilized Species*.

Jim Dunn is a poet and author of *Soft Launch* (Bootstrap, 2008), *Convenient Hole* (Pressed Wafer, 2004), and *Insects In Sex* (Falling Angel Press, 1995). His work has appeared in several publications, including *spoKe, Polis, Bright Pink Mosquito, The Process, eoagh, Gerry Mulligan, Cafe Review,* and *The Battersea Review*. He edited the poet John Wieners' journal, *A New Book From Rome*, with Derek Fenner and Ryan Gallagher of Bootstrap Press.

Michael Franco is a poet, playwright and artist. His publications include: *The Marvels of David Leering* [Pressed Wafer 2017] *A BOOK OF MEASURE Volume One: The Journals of the Man who Keeps Bees* [Talisman House 2017] *The Library Of Dr Dee,* [dromenon press for Pressed Wafer 2006], *How To Live* [Zoland, Cambridge Ma. 1998]. He was the founder of the Word of Mouth Readings Series in Cambridge Ma and currently curates the Xit The Bear reading series in Somerville MA. where he works and lives with his wife Isabel and son Thomas.

Kim Garcia is the author of *DRONE* (Backwaters Press), *Tales of the Sisters* (Sow's Ear Press), *Madonna Magdalene* (Turning Point Books) and *The Brighter House* (White Pine Press). She teaches creative writing at Boston College.

Nina Gabrielyan (b. 1953) is a widely published Moscow-based Russian Armenian poet, author, and artist. Her main poetry collections are *Trostnikovaya dudka* ("The Reed Flute," 1987),

Zerno granata ("The Pomegranate Seed," 1992), and *Poyshchee derevo* ("The Singing Tree," 2010). She is also the author of a volume of fiction, *Khoziain Travy* ("The Grass Master," 2001). Her poetic from translations several languages have been featured in 30+ collections and anthologies. Gabrielyan is a member the Moscow Writers Union and of the International Artists Foundation.

Vladimir Gandelsman, born in 1948 in Leningrad, is a widely acclaimed Russian poet and translator living in NYC. He has taught at Vassar College and Indiana University and published over a dozen collections of Russian verse and has contributed (in English translation) to the anthologies Crossing Centuries: *The New Generation of Russian Poetry* (Talisman, 2000) and *Modern Poetry in Translation: Looking Eastward #21* (King's College, London, 2003), and to many literary magazines, including The New Republic). He received the Liberty Award (2008, for fostering cultural ties between Russia and the US), and several literary awards including the Russian Prize (2008) and the Moscow Reckoning Prize (2011).

Danielle Legros Georges is a poet, translator, and educator. She is the former Boston Poet Laureate, and Director of the Lesley University MFA Program in Creative Writing.

Yuly Gugolev, born in 1964 in Moscow, is a poet, poetry translator, and TV personality. His four books of poetry are *Polnoe: Sobranie sochineniy* ("Complete: Collected Works," 2000); *Komandirovochnye predpisaniya* ("Work Tip Instructions," 2006, winner of the 2007 Moscow Reckoning Prize); *Estestvennyi otbor* ("Natural Selection," 2010); and *My – drugoy* ("We Are the Other," 2019). Gugolev's poems are translated in *Contemporary Russian Poetry: An Anthology* (Dalkey Archive Press, 2008) and in *Crossing Centuries* (Talisman, 2000).

Lisa Horowitz (B.A., M.A. Brown University; J.D. Columbia University) is an attorney and translator living and working in

New York City. In addition to *Primera causa/First Cause*, she has translated various other poems by Tino Villanueva, several of which have appeared in journals, textbooks and anthologies.

Iya Kiva was born in Donetsk, Ukraine, in 1984. She graduated from Donetsk National University. In 2014, she fled the military conflict in Donetsk and since then has lived in Kiev. Her poetry collection *Podalshe ot raya* ("Farther away from Paradise," Kyiv, 2018) was listed by PEN Ukraine in the poetry best of the year category. Her work has appeared in many literary journals in Ukraine, Russia, and elsewhere and was longlisted for the 2014 Bella and 2015 Debut literary prizes. She also writes poetry in Ukrainian.

Viktor Koval (b. 1947), of Moscow, was trained as a visual artist. He was a member of the Almanac poetry group in the later 1980s and early 1990s. Also well known as a performance artist reciting his own work, Koval has published four collections of poems and has been widely anthologized. He received the 2012 Moscow Reckoning Prize for the best poetry volume of the year.

Ruth Lepson is poet-in-residence at the New England Conservatory of Music. She recently read her poem for Cecil Taylor in a celebration of his music there. She is putting together a new & selected poems. She loves spoKe.

Elizabeth Lund writes about poetry each month for *The Washington Post*. She also reviews occasionally for *The Christian Science Monitor*, where she served as poetry editor for 10 years. Elizabeth hosts and produces Poetic Lines, which tapes outside of Boston. The show features in-depth interviews with emerging and established poets. Her own poetry has been published in the United States, Canada, and Great Britain.

Kevin McLellan is the author of *Hemispheres* (Fact-Simile Editions, 2019), *Ornitheology* (The Word Works, 2018), *[box]* (Letter [r] Press, 2016), *Tributary* (Barrow Street, 2015), and

Round Trip (Seven Kitchens, 2010). He won the 2015 Third Coast Poetry Prize and Gival Press' 2016 Oscar Wilde Award, and his poems appear in numerous literary journals including: *Colorado Review, Crazyhorse, Kenyon Review Online, West Branch, Western Humanities Review,* and *Witness.* Also, with Laura Knott, he co-wrote, co-directed, and co-produced a short experimental film titled, *Exordium.* Kevin lives in Cambridge, Massachusetts and you can find out more about him here: https://kevmclellan.com/

Evgeny Morozov was born in Nizhnekamsk, Tatarstan, Russian Federation, in 1976. He graduated from the Yelabuga State Pedagogical institute. His most recent poetry collections are *Klassicheskii zheltyj pesok* ("Classic Yellow Sand," 2014), *Kormit' ptits* ("Feed the Birds," 2016), and *O tom, kak ty byla vsegda* ("On How You Always Were," 2019). His work is also widely published in literary magazines and anthologies.

John Mulrooney is a poet, filmmaker and musician living in Cambridge, MA. He is author of *If You See Something, Say Something* from the Anchorite Press and co-producer of the documentary *The Peacemaker,* from Central Square Films. He serves as poetry editor for *Boog City.* He records and performs regularly with a number of musical groups in the greater Boston area. He is Associate Professor in the English department at Bridgewater State University. His work has appeared in *Fulcrum, Pressed Wafer fold'em zine, Solstice, the Battersea Review, Poetry Northeast, spoKe, Let the Bucket Down* and others.

Philip Nikolayev is a Russo-American bilingual poet living in Boston. He is a polyglot and translates poetry from several languages. His poetic works are published in literary periodicals internationally, including *Poetry, The Paris Review,* and *Grand Street.* Nikolayev's collections include *Monkey Time* (Verse/Wave Books) and *Letters from Aldenderry* (Salt). His translations of selected poetry by Alexander Pushkin will be brought out by Littera Publishing later this year. He co-edits *Fulcrum,* a serial anthology of poetry and critical writing.

Dennis Novikov (1967-2004), now recognized as a classic in Russia, was born and lived chiefly in Moscow, but also spent several years in England and Israel. He has influenced numerous Russian poets. Novikov attended the Literary Institute of the Writer's Union and was the youngest member of the prominent Almanac group in the 1990s. Four volumes of his poetry appeared in his lifetime. His collected poems are *Viza* ("The Visa," Voymega, Moscow, 2007). An annotated volume of Novikov's complete works, *Reka – Oblaka* ("River, Clouds"), was published by Voymega in 2019. His poems are translated into English by Philip Nikolayev with the exclusive permission of the estate of Dennis Novikov.

Alexander Pavlov, a poet, was born in the Urals in 1961. He graduated with a degree in translation from the Linguistics University of Nizhny Novgorod. He has served as a military translator, an air force pilot, and a newspaper correspondent and editor. His poems and fiction have been widely published in literary periodicals and anthologies. Pavlov's poetry books include *osin'vesna* ("fall/spring," 2012) and *nedolet* ("short of target," 2015). He lives in Armavir in the North Caucasus.

Mark Pawlak is the author of nine poetry collections and the editor of six anthologies. His latest book is *Reconnaissance: New and Selected Poems and Poetic Journals* (2016), Pawlak's poems has been translated into German, Japanese, Polish, and Spanish, and has been performed at Teatre Polski in Warsaw. His essays and memoirs have appeared in *The Woven Tale, Fusion Magazine, Jacket 2, Let the Bucket Down*, and in two anthologies, *Writers and Their Notebooks* and *Denise Levertov in Company*, both from South Carolina University Press. He teaches mathematics at the University of Massachusetts Boston to support his writing habit. He lives in Cambridge.

KL Pereira's debut short story collection, *A Dream Between Two Rivers: Stories of Liminality* was published in 2017 by Cutlass

Press. Pereira's fiction, poetry, and nonfiction appear or are forthcoming in the British Fantasy Award winning anthology *Years Best Weird Fiction vol. 5, Shadows and Tall Trees, vol. 8, Literary Hub, LampLight, The Drum, Shimmer, Innsmouth Free Press, Mythic Delirium, Jabberwocky,* and *Bitch Magazine* among others. Pereira is working on a collection of dramatic monologues called "Where Your Flames Bite My Thigh," written in the voices of women, both historical and imagined, who have been accused of witchcraft and eschewed the term "witch," and those who have embraced it. She lives in a Victorian garrett across from a haunted cemetery with her feline familiar.

Patrick Pritchett is the author of four books of poetry, most recently *Orphic Noise*. He has taught at Harvard and Hunan Normal University in Changsha, China, and currently teaches at UCONN-Hartford.

David Rich worked as the poet Gerrit Lansing's archivist from 2017 to 2018, and as archivist for Lansing's estate from 2018 to 2019. He co-edited and wrote the postscript for *Arcana: A Stephen Jonas Reader* (City Lights, 2019) and edited *Charles Olson: Letters Home, 1949 – 1969* (Cape Ann Museum, 2010). He studied archaeology at Boston University and theology at Harvard Divinity School. Rich's poems and essays have appeared in literary magazines such as *The Doris, Kadar Koli, Let the Bucket Down, No Infinite, Rain Taxi* and *Polis*.

Lisa Rosinsky was the 2016-2017 Associates of the Boston Public Library Writer-in-Residence. Her debut novel is *Inevitable and Only* (Boyds Mills Press, 2017). She is a senior editor at Barefoot Books, where she also writes picture books under the pen name Skye Silver, and she holds an MFA in poetry from Boston University, where she was a 2016 Robert Pinsky Teaching Fellow and a teaching artist at the Boston Arts Academy. Her poems have appeared in *Prairie Schooner, The Cimarron Review, Mid-American Review, Measure, 32 Poems, Hunger Mountain,* and other journals.

Charlie Steinberg is a young poet based in Boston. He's currently working on an illustrated chapbook of bad haikus written on an awful cruise. He is grateful to be debuting his work alongside so many talented poets in *spoKe 6*.

Michael Schermerhorn is a poet who lives in the belly of Boston, MA. He is currently working on his first book-length poetic study in material culture, queer artistry, and memory. His poems have previously appeared in *b(OINK), december*, and *The Penn Review*.

Born in Saint Petersburg in 1982, **Gali-Dana Singer** came to Israel in 1988. She is a poet, translator, visual artist, and coeditor (with Nekoda Singer) of the bilingual Hebrew-Russian online literary magazine *Dvoetochie / Nekudataim* ("Colon Sign"). Her poetry is anthologized in *A Sea of Voices: Women Poets in Israel* (Sherman Asher Publishing, 2008). The author of eight published volumes of Russian poetry and of four in Hebrew, she is the recipient of the Yair Tzaban 1998 Prize, of the 2000 prize awarded by the Poets Festival in Metulla, and of the Israeli Prime Minister's Prize for Hebrew Writers (2004). She has also published seven volumes of poetic translations in Russian and Hebrew.

Sunnylyn Thibodeaux's most recent books are *Universal Fall Precautions* (Spuyten Duyvil, 2017), *As Water Sounds* (Bootstrap Press, 2014) and *What's Going On* (Bird & Beckett, 2017). She lives in San Francisco with her husband Micah Ballard and their daughter Lorca. She co-edits *Auguste Press* and *Lew Gallery Editions*.

Andrei Toropoy was born in Kamensk-Uralskii in the Ural Mountains of Russia. He received an MA and a PhD in history at Urals State University and is an expert on the history of the Urals. His main poetry collections are: *Spasitelnyi nedug* ("Salutary Malady," 2005), *Stihi* ("Poems," 2008), and *Kniga stihotvorenijj* ("Book of Poems," 2012). He lives in Ekaterinburg, where he works as an archivist.

Joseph Torra is a novelist, poet, memoirist and editor. Books include My Ground Trilogy, What It Takes, What's So Funny (fiction); Keep Watching the Sky, After the Chinese, Time Being (poetry). He edited the journals lift, Let the Bucket Down, and the book Arcana: The Stephen Jonas Reader.

One of Russia's outstanding living poets, **Alexei Tsvetkov** was a co-founder, with Sergey Gandlevsky, Bakhyt Kenjeev, and Alexander Soprovsky, of the Moscow Time poetry group in the 1970s. In 1975 he was arrested and deported from Moscow for political dissidence, and in the same year he emigrated to the United States. He edited the émigré newspaper *Russkaya Zhizn* (San Francisco, 1976–77) and holds a Ph.D. degree from the University of Michigan. A long-term resident of New York City, he has recently relocated to Israel.

Meg Tyler most recent books are *Universal Fall Precautions* (Spuyten Duyvil, 2017), *As Water Sounds* (Bootstrap Press, 2014) and *What's Going On* (Bird & Beckett, 2017). She lives in San Francisco with her husband Micah Ballard and their daughter Lorca. She co-edits *Auguste Press* and *Lew Gallery Editions*.

Peter Valente is the author of *A Boy Asleep Under the Sun: Versions of Sandro Penna* (Punctum Books, 2014), which was nominated for a Lambda award, *The Artaud Variations* (Spuyten Duyvil, 2014), *Let the Games Begin: Five Roman Writers* (Talisman House, 2015), *The Catullus Versions* (Spuyten Duyvil, 2017), two books of photography, *Blue* (Spuyten Duyvil) and *Street Level* (Spuyten Duyvil, 2016), two translations from the Italian, *Blackout* by Nanni Balestrini (Commune Editions, 2017) and *Whatever the Name* by Pierre Lepori (Spuyten Duyvil, 2017), Two Novellas: *Parthenogenesis & Plague in the Imperial City* (Spuyten Duyvil, 2017), a collaboration with Kevin Killian, *Ekstasis* (blazeVOX, 2017) and the chapbook, *Forge of Words a Forest*

(Jensen Daniels, 1998). He is the co-translator of the chapbook, *Selected Late Letters of Antonin Artaud, 1945-1947* (Portable Press at Yo-Yo Labs, 2014), and has translated the work of Gérard Greek and Latin authors. Forthcoming is his translation of *Nicolas Pages* by Guillaume Dustan (Semiotext(e), 2019), and a collection de Nerval and Pier Paolo Pasolini, as well as numerous Ancient of essays, *Essays on the Peripheries* (Punctum, 2019). In 2010, he turned to filmmaking and has completed sixty shorts to date, twenty-four of which were screened at Anthology Film Archives in NYC.

Allison Vanouse is a PhD candidate at the Editorial Institute at Boston University. She lives in Cambridge, MA.

Tino Villanueva writes and also paints. He's the author of seven books of poetry. His *Scene from the Movie GIANT* (1993) won a 1994 American Book Award. Six of his poems appear in *The Norton Anthology of Latino Literature* (2011). His art work appears on the covers / inside pages of: *Green Mountains Review, TriQuarterly, Parnassus*. Latest book: *So Spoke Penelope* (2013), translated into Italian, French and Spanish. An anthology of part of his work has been translated into French, *Anthologie de Poèmes Choisis* (2015). One of his ekphrastic poems appears in the March 2016 issue of *Poetry* magazine. He recently retired from the Department of Romance Studies, Boston University.

Marc Vincenz has published fourteen books of poetry, including more recently, *Becoming the Sound of Bees, Leaning into the Infinite, The Syndicate of Water & Light,* and *Here Comes the Nightdust*. Vincenz is also a prolific translator and has translated from the German, Romanian and French. He has published ten books of translations, most recently *Unexpected Development* by award-winning Swiss poet and novelist Klaus Merz (White Pine, 2018) and which was a finalist for the 2016 Cliff Becker Book Prize in Translation. His work has received fellowships and grants from the Swiss Arts Council, the Literary Colloquium Berlin, the National Endowment for the Arts, and the Witter Bynner Foundation for Poetry.

Yanislav Wolfson originally lived in Yalta, Crimea, relocating to the US in 1990. His poems were never published during the Soviet period. In 2003 the OGI publishing house in Moscow brought out two books by him: *Yaltinskaja filma* ("Yalta Film," poems) and *Glaz vopiyushchego v pustyne* ("An Eye Crying in the Wilderness," fiction). A few more collections of his poetry books have come out since. He lives in Minnesota.